Gambling Addiction Monster

Holly Anne Ellison

Square Reads

Copyright © 2022 by Holly Anne Ellison

The content contained within this book may not be reproduced, duplicated, or transmitted without direct written permission from the author or the publisher.

Under no circumstances will any blame or legal responsibility be held against the publisher, or author, for any damages, reparation, or monetary loss due to the information contained within this book. Either directly or indirectly. You are responsible for your own choices, actions, and results.

Legal Notice:

This book is copyright protected. This book is only for personal use. You cannot amend, distribute, sell, use, quote or paraphrase any part, or the content within this book, without the consent of the author or publisher.

Disclaimer Notice:

Please note the information contained within this document is for educational and entertainment purposes only. All effort has been executed to present accurate, up-to-date, and reliable, complete information. No warranties of any kind are declared or implied.

Readers acknowledge that the author is not engaging in the rendering of legal, financial, medical or professional advice. The content within this book has been derived from various sources. Please consult a licensed professional before attempting any techniques outlined in this book.

By reading this document, the reader agrees that under no circumstances is the author responsible for any losses, direct or indirect, which are incurred as a result of the use of the information contained within this document, including, but not limited to, — errors, omissions, or inaccuracies.

978-1-7391181-4-3

First Edition

Contents

Introduction   VII
    Meet Your GAM
    Meet Me
    What's In It for You?

1. What Is Your GAM?   1
    Why Your GAM Won't Want You to Read This Book
    Why Women Fall Victim
    Embrace Your GAM
    Self-Image, Self-Esteem and Self-Confidence

2. Stereotypes and the Myths of Gambling Addiction   13
    Stereotypes
    Myths
    What You Don't Know About Compulsive Gamblers
    What An Addicted Gambler Is Really Like

3. The Big Deception   27
    Why Winning Is the Worst Thing that Can Happen to You
    Slots Manipulation and Psychology Behind It

4. The Setup   37
    Loyalty Programs
    Mixed Messages from Casinos

    Casino Design

5. Did You Inherit Your Gambling Addiction?   47
　　Is Gambling in Your Genes?
　　My Something Else
　　Addiction vs. Pastime
　　How to Recognize You Have a Gambling Problem
　　Being Susceptible to Addiction

6. Evaluate Your GAM   59
　　Your Role in the Problem
　　How Did Your GAM Take Control?
　　Clarity
　　Your Dis-Ease
　　Face Your Fear
　　Spiritual Awakening

7. Betting Your Life Away   71
　　You Will Definitely Stop Gambling

8. Time for Action   77
　　Dig Deep
　　Stop Getting Played
　　Harness Your Anger
　　First Steps First
　　Practical Steps

9. Your Future is Now   97
　　Future Self
　　Why You'll Never Be Happy with a Gambling Addiction
　　From Mindless to Mindful

10. Calm Your Urges 103
    Ideas to Calm Your Urges

11. Feel Like a True Winner 115
    Redefining Your Life on Your Terms
    Working Toward a Better You

12. Help and Support 121
    International
    United States of America
    United Kingdom
    Other Regions

Conclusion 127

References 133

Introduction

*"**Whatever you are not changing, you are choosing.**"*
- Laurie Buchanan, PhD

WHAT STARTED OUT AS fun for you has become anything but. You've found yourself trapped in a reality from which you feel there is no escape.

Like dirty clothes in the washing machine, you need to be cleaned, but all you find is that you are spinning around and drowning in an endless cycle of actual gambling, thinking about gambling, and feeling guilty for gambling.

This is no way to live, and the good news is that you absolutely don't have to.

With modern technology and change in the laws that have increased the ability to gamble online, access to gambling has never been easier. Without strict barriers in place, you can easily find yourself in a situation over which you feel you have no control.

Today it is more important than ever before to make the conscious decision to break this cycle.

Meet Your GAM

It's like entering a cave initially. It's an open cavern and you can see all around you.

Sunlight filters in through the entry point. There's nothing to be afraid of here. You spend time exploring and then see different paths leading off the main cave. These look interesting and since you've already explored the part you initially entered, you decide to venture down one of these alternate paths.

Suddenly, you feel your chosen path narrowing and the light fading. Should you turn around and go back or should you continue? You've heard fantastic things about this particular cave and decide it's well worth the risk to continue, and so you do.

As you journey down the path, you are relieved to find the space opens, and light floods in from above. You feel much better. You feel safe and are happy that you decided to continue. You pass another explorer, and they are excited about what they discovered down a different path leading off this section of the cave.

You want to see it too. You want that experience!

And so off you go, hoping you're on the same path they mentioned to you, but after a while, you have doubts because you're not seeing everything you were told about. You see another passage and take that, then another and another as you search for the cavern you were told about. It's getting dark and narrow again and now it's rather damp too, and the smell is unpleasant.

You hadn't planned on this.

Again, what do you do?

It could be too late to go back, and you possibly don't even know the way, and although the odds are on your side to retrace your steps back to safety, something else is telling you to continue, just a little bit further, you're almost there. Don't give up now, just before you are about to reach your goal.

And so, against your better judgment, you continue into the unknown, aware of the high risk.

The sides of the passage are pressing against you now, and you're finding it difficult to move. The urge to run is overwhelming, but you are stuck and unable to break free.

You are startled by an unexpected noise, but it's more than that. It's like a deep roar. You feel frightened and trapped, and so you should.

You've finally met your GAM, and now you are entirely at its mercy.

This whole situation and feeling is so unexpected. You feel terrified and excited all at the same time. Your emotions are a mess, and your thoughts are all over the place.

What on earth are you doing here?

How did you get yourself into this awful situation?

Then all goes quiet, and your GAM smiles at you. You think you see it wink too, but you're not sure. It starts to whisper, and its voice no longer sounds like something outside of you but rather something within. And although it's an unfamiliar whisper, it's very reassuring and understanding.

Yes, it knows exactly what you are looking for and promises to help you get there. You take its hand, feel compelled to listen to it, and follow wherever it leads.

You completely surrender your own logic and reasoning and put all your faith into your GAM.

And almost as suddenly as you found yourself in this dark passage, you escape. You feel the sunlight on your face, you can breathe again and life feels wonderful.

You are happy that you met your GAM, you are thankful you listened, and you are grateful for that experience.

You know the next time you hear it; you will listen again. You want to repeat that incredible experience it showed you and wonder where else it will take you.

You don't realize that you are becoming an addicted gambler, but you are. Your GAM has already got its hooks into you and intends to use you in whatever way it can to satisfy its own needs.

As its hold on you gets stronger and stronger, you begin to lose parts of yourself. It seems that you give away these parts so easily. These parts may not be perfect, but they are part of you, and more natural to you than your GAM will ever be.

But at this time, you simply don't believe it. You've lost touch and feel you've become your GAM. You think you are your addiction. It's who you've become, who you now are.

And this misguided belief holds you in that never-ending cycle, forever in the wash cycle, unable to get clean.

INTRODUCTION　　xi

Meet Me

With a fresh perspective, understanding, and a relentless desire to change, you can finally slay your GAM and fulfill your desire to win.

But first, allow me to introduce myself. My name is Holly Anne Ellison, and I am a recovered compulsive gambler with decades-long severe gambling addiction to slots. I understand first-hand what it's like to suffer from this awful addiction and how difficult it is to overcome.

The ideas and solutions expressed in this book are merely my own and are offered with the hope that if they worked for me, they could work for you too. If you are undergoing professional treatment for your addiction, my ideas should be used after first consulting with your therapist or counselor, neither of which I am.

If you've read my short book, *Fear of Gambling Addiction Recovery*, you will have a better understanding of who I am and more insight into the depth of my addiction. And if you haven't, let me tell you, it was bad.

When I think back on those days, I cringe. I don't recognize myself, but I have self-compassion because I didn't know what I know now.

For many years gambling was my thing. I was addicted to playing casino slots, specifically certain slot games, with one game in particular and also the same slot machine that game was on, which was situated at the end of the row where I could pretty much play undisturbed from the public at large.

Of course, over time, other regulars got to know me, and I got to know other players too, primarily women, who would regularly play in that row of machines. We would cheer each other on and take pleasure in each other's wins, and when I experienced decent wins, there were usually a group of other regular players there to congratulate me. It seemed I wasn't alone in my obsession.

This social aspect became part of my gambling experience. I didn't have many close friends near me, and this was my way of connecting with other like-minded individuals. We became kindred spirits but really knew nothing about each other. Gambling was our only connection.

Although I was married with grown-up children, I see today that at heart, I was a lonely soul. I had some wonderful friends I had known since childhood, but they all lived in different countries, and I had lost touch with them for a long time. In the earlier days of my gambling habit, it was too expensive to make international phone calls to stay in touch, and I never was much good at letter writing.

Of course, when the technology was developed to enjoy free facetime calls, I was able to reconnect. As much as I loved having my old friends back in my life, it was more about catching up when we spoke than actually having them there in my life to share experiences with.

The casino continued to be my special place, and my gambling acquaintances continued to be my special people.

How sad was that?

It's not easy sharing this part, but I feel it's essential because, at that time, my addiction was being formed. Other factors, apart from the excitement and thrills of winning, conditioned me to associate the casino environment with experiencing friendship and feeling special. Of course, there were no real friendships, and the casino was simply the place that hooked me in.

I wasted thousands of dollars and hours of my life I will never get back. I am not only referring to the time I spent gambling but the time I spent thinking about it and not fully appreciating what I had and what I was experiencing when I wasn't at the casino.

But it's never too late.

I finally managed to turn everything around. Coming up with the Gambling Addiction Monster was a game changer for me, and it's the foundation of this book. Just as I finally overcame my addiction, I truly believe you can do so too.

What's In It for You?

The short answer is *EVERYTHING*.

I know that asking you to trust me is a big ask because you don't even trust yourself and your judgment.

If you're reading this book, there is hope that you can fully recover and turn your life around. You're reading this book with the expectation that somewhere within you will find the magic recipe that will finally set you free.

To be honest, I will tell you right now that this book has no magic recipe. The magic that you need is within you and always has been. You haven't felt it in so long that you've forgotten it exists. You've been looking to fill that empty space with everything outside, which never works in the long run.

But all is not lost, yet.

Believe me when I tell you the magic is there. Bring that to your recovery. You will clear the path for your magic to flow by firstly deciding to get better and do better.

By continuing to read this book, you will better understand the factors that contributed to your gambling addiction and the practical solutions that will help you overcome it.

And as long as you're gambling, you will only experience more of the same issues, worries, and guilt.

As I write these words in this book today, I have been clean for over three years, and it's the best feeling ever. The ultimate jackpot is to continually experience those days of clarity that I would enjoy in between my gambling sessions.

Although it hasn't always been easy, I finally have peace of mind. I know who I am and exactly where I am headed, and I believe I'll get there because now I can trust myself.

Without throwing money away on gambling, I have been able to enjoy many special times that, if I had still been gambling, I would not have gotten to do. These included fabulous overseas family vacations and an exceptional trip to spend time with my oldest and dearest friend; one who genuinely cared about me and with whom I had so much in common even though we are very different. A real friend.

It would have been wonderful to have made that trip earlier, but when I was gambling, and I had that thought, it was instantly dismissed as too expensive. And, of course, we all know why.

You should be excited about your future. I want you to be hopeful about the possibilities you are about to face. Even if you've tried unsuccessfully before to turn your back on gambling, it's not too late to try again. And it's definitely worthwhile.

As an addicted gambler, you've never walked away from an opportunity to win; now is not the time to start.

It's now time to place one last bet, this time on yourself.

And this time, you may even win the ultimate jackpot: your peace of mind, sanity, clarity, trust in yourself, self-respect, and financial stability.

In other words, your life!

But before you can permanently slay your GAM, you need to understand it.

And before you can understand it, you need to get to know it.

Chapter 1

What Is Your GAM?

"Addiction begins with the hope that something "out there" can instantly fill up the emptiness inside."
- Jean Kilbourne

EVERY COMPULSIVE GAMBLER IS saddled with their own Gambling Addiction Monster (GAM) that controls their urge to gamble and overrides their own reasoning power with irrational thoughts that compel them to gamble even when they know better.

Until now, you've probably considered your gambling addiction part of you.

This will remain true if you believe you are your gambling addiction and can't control *yourself*.

By separating yourself from your GAM you can begin to get back control.

Recognizing the GAM as a separate entity, like a parasite living within you, is the first step towards recovery.

2   GAMBLING ADDICTION MONSTER

When you identify your GAM and understand that it is not you, you can begin making decisions and taking action that is coming from *you*, for you.

You are not actually denying yourself something.

You are denying your GAM, who is not you.

YOU:

- Want to feel good inside in an authentic and natural way
- You don't want to feel tired, guilty, and broke
- You are sick of feeling stressed and trapped
- You want to feel like a real winner in life
- You want to be in control

YOUR GAM:

- Wants to feel good no matter the cost
- Your GAM doesn't think about consequences
- Your GAM never feels negative about gambling
- When you lose, your GAM just goes away while you are left to pick up pieces.
- Your GAM wants to be in control.

Part of a compulsive gambler's problem is that they identify with being a gambler. It is who they are, and it's difficult to give up part of yourself; after all, that is you.

But it is not you.

Giving up gambling should be seen as moving away from something negative and toward something positive.

You will move away from your GAM and towards the best version of yourself.

When you give up something, you are creating a space in your life for something better, something genuine and sustainable.

As long as that space is filled with gambling, you will not have the inclination, time, or resources to achieve anything else of value or meaning.

The common element between you and your GAM is that you both want control. Those inner battles that take place are where you both try to get control of the other.

These are the battles you usually lose and, up until now, thought you were battling yourself.

Gamblers have times of clarity. These times the GAM is dormant, and you are in control of yourself. You know what you want to do, what you want to achieve.

You know what is right and wrong.

During this time, you must implement as much as possible to overcome your addiction without interference from your GAM.

You must decide whether you want to be free of your GAM and addiction. If so, immediately do what you can when your mind is clear and in control.

Why Your GAM Won't Want You to Read This Book

Your GAM doesn't care about you.

Like a parasite, it only needs you to enable its ability to feed. If you stop feeding it, it will gradually get quieter and quieter until it ceases to exist, and you will finally be free.

Nobody wants to be food for a parasite.

According to the Miriam-Webster dictionary, a parasite is described as *"an organism living in, on, or with another organism in order to obtain nutrients, grow, or multiply often in a state that directly or indirectly harms the host."* (*Definition of Parasite*, 2022), (in this case this host is you).

So, you are the host, and your GAM is the organism living off you. And just as with a physical parasite, this mental parasite is doing precisely the same thing to you in that it is causing you harm.

This is both physical and mental harm.

Besides the vast releases of dopamine into your system, which put your hormonal balances out whack, the continued stress from financial losses and internal battles adversely affects your mental health.

In the case of an addicted gambler, the parasite cannot be seen. It is an invisible enemy who can only be heard. It resides in your brain, hijacking your thoughts, free will, and judgment.

The more you listen to the voice of your GAM instead of your own, the louder and more potent it becomes, leaving you feeling helpless and trapped. You get caught in a cycle which spirals out of control unless you, the host, do something about it. As the host, you do have the power to take active steps to eliminate your GAM. You just need to believe you can and learn how to do this.

Your GAM understands that by reading this book, you will acquire the knowledge to slay it and stop gambling. As it certainly doesn't want you to stop gambling, it will use every weapon in its arsenal against you. It doesn't want you to get help and will be very tricky in the messages it sends you.

These messages will include reasons you don't want to quit gambling and objections to continue reading the book.

This will be your first opportunity to ignore your GAM. This is where you can begin taking back some control.

Why Women Fall Victim

Women can be lonely. They can drive to a casino and feel relaxed entering it on their own, whereas most would not feel comfortable spending considerable time in a bar or restaurant alone. Because many other women are doing the same thing, they meet with others like themselves, get to know regulars and make "friends".

They are not worried about standing out alone because the casino is full of single chairs for players to gamble alone. This is somewhere they can easily blend in and feel relatively safe.

Women are often in control of the household finances. They plan the meals and do the shopping, so it's easy for them to skim off the top to feed the slot machine.

This whole thing becomes an emotional experience, and when you get into the gambling zone while playing slots, it is like being on a roller coaster that you cannot get off, despite how scary it is and no matter how much you wish you could. You have to stay until the ride is over.

When you're in that zone, the world is blocked out. It is just you and your chosen slot machine or game. You become automated. Your actions are robotic. Your breathing changes. It can be shallow, like almost holding your breath, or fast, depending upon what is happening in your session.

When you play a slot game that you know really well, this can be more amplified. You know exactly the value of each symbol on the reel and what you need to succeed. As you press the spin button each time, your eyes dart from left to right at the speed of light to see if this will be the one. Within a millisecond, you see it is not, and you press the button again and repeat and repeat until everything is gone.

In between, you may experience some good lines, and for a short time, you hope it will be different this time. This time you will win, or at the very least, you will not lose.

And of course, the whole experience is amplified by sounds, music, and lighting.

With modern technology, many no longer need to leave their homes to gamble. A quick session can be accessed from your laptop or phone while you're waiting for the washing to dry, dinner to cook, or even sitting in your car waiting for your children to finish school.

When other parts of your life are not satisfying, or you are in a dysfunctional relationship where you have no overall control, gambling also gives you the illusion of control. It's important to understand that's all it is, an illusion.

You think *you* decided to gamble.

You believe you can control how much money you spend, but as time goes on, you soon realize this is not the case which causes you to spiral even more.

And if you're gambling from home, you can consume alcohol easily without having to concern yourself with drinking and driving.

With the consumption of more alcohol, your resistance to gambling will be even lower, as will your impulse control.

Gambling is also so easy to hide. Unlike other addictions like alcohol or substance abuse, where it is evident that a person is drunk or high, to the untrained eye, it is not apparent that you are a compulsive gambler.

And with hiding the gambling addiction, your GAM has all the time it needs to grow, get stronger, and entirely consume you.

Embrace Your GAM

Now that I've introduced you to the GAM concept, it's time to embrace your own GAM. The most successful way of overcoming something is to tackle it head-on.

Don't be afraid to face your GAM as fear gives it control over you.

"Have you ever had one of those dreams where a dark, scary figure is chasing you? If you run away, it always gets much more terrifying. If you turn around and face it, something good almost always happens." (Michels & Stutz, 2017)

Although your GAM has got you into difficult situations, knowing that your GAM has been controlling you for so long should be a relief. With knowledge comes power, and it is now time for you to acquire the knowledge you need to get the power to overcome your addiction.

I want to clarify that the GAM is not meant as an excuse to justify your continued gambling. Once the cat is out of the bag, so to speak, you can't put it back, and now that you are fully aware of your GAM, you need to deal with it, and it is only you who can do so.

In a later chapter, I will discuss in-depth and practical steps and solutions to help you defeat your GAM, but in the meantime, you need to take some time to think about what your GAM means to you.

What makes your GAM unique to you?

1. When did you first lose control to your GAM?

2. How often does your GAM stop by?

3. How does your GAM control you?

4. What arguments does your GAM use against you?

5. Does your GAM always use arguments, or does it sometimes completely just take you over?

6. What arguments are most effective against you?

7. How would you feel if your GAM went away?

These are some guiding questions to help you better understand what's happening inside you when it comes to gambling.

Additionally, it's essential to understand the times your GAM can be most effective against you. Even with a gambling compulsion, there are times when you think about it but can dismiss the idea, and then, of course, there are those times when you simply don't stand a chance.

You need to explore why that is, so that you can take evasive and defensive steps.

What is your frame of mind or mood when your GAM is able to easily control you?

Possibilities can include:

- When you're tired

- When you feel pressure to make money

- When you have more money

- When you've had a bad day and feel stressed

- When you've had a good day and want to celebrate

Although addicted gamblers seldom need an excuse to go gambling, and anytime is a good time to do so, the above possibilities are potential situations where your GAM can be more persuasive than usual.

When you are aware of these times, you can implement specific actions because being fore-warned enables you to become fore-armed.

Self-Image, Self-Esteem and Self-Confidence

In research from Faillace (2021), "t*he way we view ourselves can play a big part in the things we do and our interactions with others. Self-image, self-esteem, and self-confidence are all important pieces to helping us see how great we can be. When these pieces are misaligned, we might feel bad about ourselves or think we are not good enough."*

We know compulsive gambling harms our self-image, self-esteem, and self-confidence. And despite knowing this, we continue.

Until, of course, one day we stop, and how we stop is discussed in detail in the chapter Betting Your Life Away.

We all know that to live productive, healthy, and happy lives, we must be at peace. We need to have a good self-image, have high self-esteem, and value and trust in ourselves.

It's impossible to feel joy, happiness, or success when the shadow of your GAM looms overhead. Our struggle will continue if these three criteria are off balance or missing. Other areas of our lives will suffer too.

The GAM has to go.

To succeed with your mission, you need to feel in control and have the confidence in yourself that you will be able to do this and that it will be worthwhile.

As your self-confidence has already been stripped back because of your compulsive gambling and the lack of trust you have in yourself and your own judgment, this is how separating yourself from your GAM is truly helpful.

When you separate yourself from your GAM, it's like getting a temporary reprieve where your self-image, self-esteem, and self-confidence are higher than they've been in a long, long time.

I use the word temporary because this increase in positive feelings only relates to your GAM and how you deal with it. Further work is required to fully recover and enjoy these positive traits permanently.

Your self-image improves because you realize you are not your gambling addiction. You have been targeted and enslaved by your GAM. You have been a victim of an all-consuming parasite.

You no longer see *yourself* as the addicted gambler, but rather a victim of this insatiable parasite. And because nobody wants to be a victim, this is something you will want to, and can remedy.

An increase in your self-esteem comes next. You not only recognize and understand what has been going on within you, but when you accept this and decide to do something about it and take action, you will feel a boost in your self-esteem.

Boosting your self-esteem will lead to a natural increase in self-confidence, which is paramount to slaying our GAM once and for all.

Gamblers are often misunderstood, and that's not at all surprising. If we battle to understand our own addiction, how can we expect society at large or those we love to understand?

And if we're not going to be understood but rather harshly judged, why would we want to discuss the problem with anyone?

Nobody wants to feel worse than they already do, so we just keep quiet and are left completely isolated, struggling with our gambling addiction alone.

With this in mind, let's look closely at some myths about gambling addiction.

Chapter 2

Stereotypes and the Myths of Gambling Addiction

"I'm a big fan of the misunderstood, the vilified, the underdog, the breaking of myths."
- Dominic Monaghan

NOBODY WANTS TO BE a stereotype, and you aren't one. Everybody has problems and how they evolve and culminate depends on various factors. You are a unique individual whose issues have evolved over time, culminating in gambling addiction.

- Location
- Finances
- Gender
- Stability

- Personality
- Beliefs
- Upbringing
- Education
- History

People with the same fundamental problems can become afflicted with different behaviors or addictions. For example, some will turn to alcohol or drugs, some will become compulsive gamblers, some will never be faithful, and others will become shopaholics or have diet issues, and today social media junkies, and on the other end of the scale are those that become violent offenders and even murderers.

And just as there is no stereotype for murderers, there is also no stereotype for an addicted gambler. Anybody could be one. If every murdered victim immediately recognized their killer as a murderer, homicide rates would be far lower.

Unfortunately, this isn't the case.

For far too long, gambling addicts have been viewed as degenerates with no moral compass.

Stereotypes

Typical stereotypes include:

- Only Older People Gamble

- Most Gamblers Are or Will Become Criminals
- Men Gamble More Than Women
- Gamblers Are Lazy
- Gamblers Should Get a Job
- They Are Desperate and Out of Control
- The Poor Are More Likely to Gamble
- Educated and Intelligent People Don't Gamble

Only Older People Gamble

Gambling is available in legitimate casinos anywhere in the world to those of legal age. People of all ages and from all walks of life visit casinos and, under the right circumstances, can become addicted.

The days are long gone when this was something you only did when you retired.

Most Gamblers Are or Will Become Criminals

Of course, some gamblers are criminals, just like anybody with any hobby or occupation could be a criminal, but this is not the characteristic of most gamblers.

Most compulsive gamblers are guilty of making poor decisions, displaying lousy judgment, and risking their financial stability and peace of mind, but these are not crimes.

Addicted gamblers who turn to crime to finance their habit are not the norm.

Men Gamble More Than Women

According to research (Women Make Up Majority of Gambling-Addicted Swedes for First Time Ever, 2019), *"In the US the gender gap has been narrowing for some time - and women already slightly outnumber men in the 45-64 age group."*

Gamblers Are Lazy

Most gamblers are not lazy. It takes a tremendous effort and a lot of energy to maintain their habit, whether juggling their finances or time to ensure everything is in order to remove any potential obstacles that could stop them from gambling.

Gamblers Should Get a Job

Gamblers need money to feed their addiction, live, and care for their families. Without a job, they would be unable to do this. Access to funds and income is part of the addicted gamblers' ability to keep gambling.

They Are Desperate and Out of Control

Without a complete understanding of what it actually means to be an addicted gambler, compulsive gamblers can be seen as weak and desperate with no self-control. Society does not understand why they simply don't control themselves because they don't realize how complicated the actual problem is.

The Poor Are More Likely to Gamble

Gambling addiction is not a money issue. It's filling an emotional need that anybody could have. Access to money for excessive gambling is needed, which the wealthy are more likely to be prone to.

However, poorer people are more likely to buy lottery tickets and scratch cards when they can do so.

Educated and Intelligent People Don't Gamble

Educated and intelligent people are just as susceptible to compulsive behavior as anybody else. Even though they logically have the intelligence to know better, being addicted makes it challenging to stop. However, with proper education on the subject of gambling, they can recover.

Now, as an addicted gambler, you know the above is not valid.

Because of this stereotype, it is hard to admit to the problem because as soon as you do, you know that others will think of you with stereotypical characteristics.

The gambling addict is seen differently from other addicts because the depth of the problem is not fully understood by most. Instead of being viewed with compassion, gamblers are viewed with disdain and contempt.

It's essential to break the stereotypical image because as long as society has this view, it is harder for many to admit to their problem and seek the help they desperately need.

Addicts are already feeling low; the last thing they need is unwarranted and misinformed judgment.

We didn't all start out as gambling addicts.

And those people who may judge you today have the potential of becoming an addict tomorrow.

Myths

This complete lack of understanding is further perpetuated by gambling myths.

- Gamblers Make Bank
- Teens Don't Gamble
- You Can Always Win Your Money Back
- Only Irresponsible People Have Gambling Addictions
- Gambling Isn't a Real Addiction
- It's Only an Addiction If You Gamble Every Day
- Your Odds Will Increase If You Know the Game
- Gambling Is Only a Financial Problem
- If You Feel Lucky You Will Win
- It's Easy to Spot a Compulsive Gambler
- Gambling Is Just Harmless Fun
- Gambling Addiction Can't Be Treated

Addicted gamblers know the absolute truth behind these myths, and it's time most people do too.

As long as these myths are perpetuated, society will not understand the complexities of gambling addiction and the addict will continue to be misjudged.

Gamblers Make Bank

Although there are some exceptions to this statement, most gamblers are losers. Over time, those favored by lady luck will join the rest and continue to throw good money after bad.

Teens Don't Gamble

In the USA, 21 is the legal gambling age. However, in some states, placing bets is allowed at 18 in tribal casinos or on cruise ships. In the UK, 18 is the legal age for gambling.

However, much younger people often participate in gambling, and it can be facilitated by family members who see it as harmless fun by placing sports bets or buying scratch cards.

You Can Always Win Your Money Back

This is one of the biggest gambling myths and most dangerous. Chasing losses with the hope of winning your money back is a common trait among compulsive gamblers.

The hope that if they deposit more money, they will finally win and get everything back is a characteristic that separates fun gambling from problem gambling.

Only Irresponsible People Have Gambling Addictions

The ability that addicted gamblers have to keep their addiction hidden for so long is that they are responsible for the big things like feeding their family, going to work, or paying their mortgage.

They know that once these slide, their game will be up, and the last thing they want is to be out of the game.

Gambling Isn't a Real Addiction

If alcohol and drug addiction is real, so is gambling. All are dependent upon substance abuse.

The only difference is that alcohol and drugs are consumed from outside the body, whereas the gambler's substance, dopamine, is created by the body itself.

It's Only an Addiction If You Gamble Every Day

Addicted gamblers don't gamble every day or even every week. However, another characteristic of the addicted gambler is that even when they're not gambling, they are constantly thinking about it. When they have the opportunity to gamble, they will do so.

Your Odds Will Increase If You Know the Game

The only game that has some level of skill to it is Blackjack. However, over time, the house always wins. It's as simple as that.

Gambling Is Only a Financial Problem

Financial loss and even ruin is the obvious problem as it is money you are seen to be gambling with.

What is not seen is the lack of trust, loss of time spent with family and friends, and waste of energy that should be spent on something worthwhile.

If You Feel Lucky You Will Win

This would be a wonderful thing. Unfortunately, feeling lucky often drives gamblers to risk even more because they are convinced the payoff is coming.

It's Easy to Spot a Compulsive Gambler

The only time a compulsive gambler is visible is by examining their deposits and losses, which will tell an accurate tale of what is occurring over time. When you see somebody losing, this doesn't mean they are compulsive gamblers; the same can be said about winners.

Gambling Is Just Harmless Fun

While most people can go to the casino and enjoy a fun night out without it becoming a problem, this is how the compulsive gambler started. The harmless night out became an addiction that has taken over their lives.

Gambling Addiction Can't Be Treated

The good news is that this simply isn't true. If an addict genuinely wants recovery, numerous facilities, programs, and treatments are available, including cognitive behavioral therapy. However, many do recover on their own.

It is important to understand that people addicted to gambling do recover. They often do this completely on their own, without any treatment, as in the case of my own recovery.

> *"Pathological gambling may not always follow a chronic and persisting course. A substantial portion of individuals with a history of pathological gambling eventually recover, most without formal treatment."* (Slutske, 2006)

With a better understanding of gambling myths and stereotypes, the addicted gambler themself can be better understood.

With understanding, help can be provided because the fear of being judged will no longer be there to hinder the asking for help.

What You Don't Know About Compulsive Gamblers

Compulsive gamblers keep their actual gambling losses a secret. Friends and family may know they enjoy gambling, and some may think they visit the casino more often than most, but they are unaware of the extent of the problem because gamblers don't tell them how often they go and how much they spend.

Gambling addicts will tell people about their wins only. This sounds like the person is lucky, and others can be quite envious. But this is not the whole truth.

Sometimes gambling can be enabled by a partner. This is not to blame them because they are unaware of the extent of the problem and just see it as something you enjoy. Therefore, they will take you or encourage you to go on occasions that are not really appropriate.

Gamblers will look for any excuse to gamble. If they are happy and want to celebrate something, the casino will be an excellent place to do this. If stressed, they need to unwind and take their minds off issues, which can be done in the casino. So, no matter how you feel, the casino is always the option you go for, and there's always a reason to go.

Gamblers are constantly thinking about their next visit. Even as they leave, they are thinking about when they will be back and how much money they will have, where can they save money to keep gambling. Do they have money they can move around, etc.? This is constant stress and no way to live.

If you have your own bank account with money nobody else has visibility to, nobody will see how much you spend, and you can keep it secret. If you gamble online, nobody even knows you're there.

You will save from buying anything that will lessen your gambling pot. You will buy cheaper food items and household goods. You hardly ever spend money on clothes or makeup and would rather go to the casino than have a pedicure (although if you could afford both, then even better). You lose the pleasure in everyday shopping and feeling good about yourself.

The worst is using money on credit cards for gambling because once you've lost it, you still have to pay the money back to your credit card provider, often with interest, which compounds your loss.

What An Addicted Gambler Is Really Like

Now that I've discussed the common myths and stereotypes of gamblers, and what some gamblers can be like, I would like to share from my own experience what it feels like to be a compulsive gambler. This is not aimed at the gambler, as they are fully aware of what this hell is like, but more at family members or friends of addicted gamblers to bring real awareness to the reality of the problem.

We are normal people. We are mothers, wives, sisters, and daughters. We have responsibilities and jobs. We take care of our families. We could even be you.

At first, there was the truth. We talked about our casino visits, games we played, our wins, and even our losses. We were having fun in those days. We weren't overspending. We weren't being deceitful. We were honest with ourselves and others. That is the truth.

And then came deceit. As terrible as lying to loved ones is, the lies we tell ourselves are the worst. We don't deliberately lie. We tell ourselves something that we desperately want to believe, and we say it with an honest heart and good intent. We need to believe in ourselves. We want to keep the promises we make.

We know we have a problem deep down but seldom say it out loud. Everything is internalized. Our fears, worries, and guilt torment us. We constantly feel stressed and are usually able to hide it well.

How am I going to make it to the end of the month? How am I going to get the money to get through? Can I take on extra work? Should I borrow it?

Somehow, we make it through. We promise ourselves again that next month will be different. We will not allow ourselves to get into that hellish situation again. We are done. That was the last time. We even feel relieved.

These promises are made when we are calm and thinking clearly. We could do better and put things right. We can save. We think deeply about things and are even excited at the prospect of this change.

And then, without warning, the GAM appears. We can be washing the dishes, chatting to a friend, working, driving, anything but gambling, behaving as people without addictions do. And that's where it all stops, and everything falls apart again.

Our good intentions, promises, ability to think clearly and trust our own judgment, and our own power of reasoning are gone.

And within the fastest possible time, we find ourselves placing bets and pushing buttons again.

We become moody and snap at people for no reason. This is an outer manifestation of what's happening inside us when the urge to gamble strikes and we cannot fulfill it.

We should. We shouldn't. We want to. We don't want. We promised, but…….

These moments are absolute torture fueled by our physical need for dopamine and edged on by our GAM. We know that if we gamble, there's a chance we will get that dopamine hit, and when we do, we feel on top of the world.

And because we feel on top of the world, we want this wonderful feeling to continue. It's great to feel so good again after all the stress and guilt, so we want to enjoy this feeling for as long as possible, so when most people would walk away with a win, we don't.

We gamble everything on getting another hit.

But that doesn't happen. Instead, we lose everything again and feel worse than before going to the casino. And we hate that feeling. Once again, we are racked with shame and guilt and often self-disgust. We know we have another problematic month in front of us.

We've let ourselves down again.

And we promise ourselves, never ever again. And the sad thing is, we genuinely believe it. And to make matters worse, just as much as we deceive ourselves, we are also being deceived and manipulated by the casinos.

Chapter 3

The Big Deception

> *"The art of pleasing is the art of deception."*
> - Luc de Clapiers

THE TWINKLING LIGHTS AND sound effects from the slot machines, the soft floor lighting, and even the smell of the casino all contribute to heightening your senses when you walk in. That feeling of anticipation where you believe anything is possible is how you are supposed to feel.

The best marketing minds in the world have been used to first lure you in and then entice you to stay. With access to player data and statistics, these marketing gurus know exactly how to do this. You are exactly where they want you to be, doing exactly what they want you to do.

You have been deceived twice.

Your GAM has led you down the garden path to the casino, and when you get there, you are further manipulated and deceived by the casino setup.

Why Winning Is the Worst Thing that Can Happen to You

To a gambling addict, there is no better feeling than a decent win. Often, this kind of win is not significant and will reinforce that you are possibly on the verge of hitting it big. Unfortunately, apart from those rare exceptions, this is just what the casinos want you to believe.

Instead of cashing out, content with winning your money back and not actually losing, you will continue to play, perhaps even increasing your bet so that when the perfect line appears on the slot reel, you will win big.

You will probably play this out. Slots give you wins only to take it back. You may think if you deposit more money, you will definitely win.

There are only two winners in this situation, and you are not one of them. The first is the casino. They manipulated you into believing this was your lucky day and you were about to win big, and the second winner is your GAM. That win when it happened felt good, and don't you want to experience that again? Your GAM now has another weapon in its arsenal to manipulate you further down the road.

And if you do happen to experience a huge win, well, you've now had a taste of it and been left with an insatiable hunger for more.

The worst winning experience happened to me at a small land-based casino while on holiday. I wasn't much into water sports, so this was the perfect opportunity for me to go off and do my thing.

My whole family was out on the water, having fun, and of course, I was in the casino on my own.

I had limited funds, so I needed my money to last a good few hours. I knew I wouldn't be able to withdraw additional money as I needed to ensure I had sufficient for the family to enjoy themselves, so I needed to win to enjoy my holiday doing what I did.

Right away, it didn't look very promising. I was playing a slots game I loved. I had started on one machine, which was dead. Nothing was happening. No decent lines, no free spins, so I moved a few machines down to another machine of the same game.

Although this machine played slightly better, it was still draining my funds but a little slower. After about half an hour on that second machine, I was down to my last ten dollars. I could feel the stress building up. I didn't want to end up with nothing. I wanted to be able to continue playing in the casino for as long as possible as I had planned to do. I didn't even mind if it took all my money when it would be time for me to leave to meet my family and go for a meal. I just wanted it to last until then.

But as I pressed the button each time and watched those reels spin, the inevitable loss was becoming more and more apparent. I had already reduced my bet to stretch my funds out but did this again. I made a few more bets and then, as I was down to my last three dollars, I told myself to go big or go home. There wasn't much risk in this because even at the minimum bet, there were only a few more presses of the button till I would be wiped out and would have to leave anyway.

So, I increased my bet, betting all I had on one last push of that button and I couldn't believe it.

I got a free spin. And within that spin and I got two more. And I hit a full line. Wow!

I had done it. I won over a thousand dollars!

And of course, with that win, which was so unexpected, I was able to continue playing that day and had enough to play for the duration of our holiday.

At no time did I even consider keeping it and taking it home.

This winning experience became ammunition for my GAM to use against me in the future. When deciding whether to withdraw more money, my GAM would always remind me how just one more press of that button could turn everything around.

Because I knew this possibility was true, it was tough to argue against it.

What I thought at the time was a remarkable win, in the long run, was anything but.

Of course, there were other good days that were fruitful and fun. However, there were bad days too, and unfortunately, there were more of those than I care to remember.

On those days, all the money I had available to gamble with would be lost. This would often mean that not only had the budgeted amount been lost, but extra money that I had rationalized to spend too. I would have made numerous trips to the ATM (called this the walk of shame) to get more money, and when my daily withdrawal limits were reached, I would go to the cashier to withdraw directly from my bank card.

The awful feelings experienced after losses like this were the lowest of the low. I would spend hours beating myself up for being so stupid, promising myself I would never ever do that again, and feel sick in my stomach.

Of course, as time passed by, these feelings would lessen. Life had gone on, and I would start to feel the urge to go gambling again.

Maybe I could win my money back?

I would tell myself everything I needed to hear (or my GAM would), to justify another trip to the casino, and off I would go again to repeat the same experience I had had before.

In a land casino, you get to see others win. Of course, you also get to see others lose, but you don't focus on that. Shame for them, but that is not you. Not today.

When you see somebody in a casino win, you see their joy. You see the admiration they get from other players. They are envied.

They did it, so why can't I?

They are happy to win the money, but it is far more than that. You see how they lap up the attention, and for a short while, they relish in the spotlight, feeling everything was worthwhile, feeling special, and adored.

You will never know how much that win has cost that person either financially in money they have spent before or in time lost that could have negatively impacted their relationships or career etc.

All you see is a winner, and you want to be one too.

Slots Manipulation and Psychology Behind It

Psychological factors are involved that play a huge role in how we behave. This struggle is then amplified by the manipulation of the casinos.

Cognitive Dissonance

If you've been battling to understand your behavior and the actions that keep you in the perpetual cycle of gambling, it's important to understand what cognitive dissonance is and how it impacts the addicted gambler.

> *"The term cognitive dissonance is used to describe the mental discomfort that results from holding two conflicting beliefs, values, or attitudes."* (Cherry, 2022)

Following through with our gambling even though we don't want to, is a sign that we are suffering from cognitive dissonance. We distance ourselves from the reality we know to be true by denying anything that supports the problem. For example, you may deny how much money you spend. You gamble in secret because you don't want others to know and because you feel guilty and ashamed.

Furthermore, Cherry (2022) goes on to say: *"The more dissonant (clashing) thoughts you have, the greater the strength of the dissonance."*

Because we are addicted gamblers, we suffer, often in silence. Our suffering is due to the constant internal conflict we feel about our gambling habits. We want to stop. We are tired of feeling this way. However, every argument we put up in the ongoing battle causes the dissonance to increase, resulting in the very behavior we are so desperate to avoid.

It's the internal battle that is the hardest to live with. We lose the internal battle and invariably also incur financial losses. It's all part of the addiction cycle.

The negative impact of cognitive dissonance is that it increases feelings of self-loathing, which consequently affects our self-esteem.

It was much easier when I envisioned those internal arguments with my GAM than with myself because I immediately eliminated the feeling that I was betraying myself. Even though my gambling actions were initially the same, the fact that it wasn't myself that had talked me into it went a long way to the positive image I began to view of myself.

Raised Dopamine Levels with Every Spin

"When you gamble, your brain releases dopamine, the feel-good neurotransmitter that makes you feel excited. You'd expect to only feel excited when you win, but your body produces this neurological response even when you lose." (The Science behind Gambling, n.d.)

Just as you can't control the release of adrenalin into your system when you find yourself in a life-threatening situation, the release of dopamine also cannot be controlled, although outside circumstances and your reaction to them, will determine how much is released.

You become hooked on the release of high dopamine doses triggered by your gambling. In the beginning, you simply enjoyed the fun of gambling, which made you feel good as many fun activities do.

However, over time, this changed. Gambling became the only activity that released dopamine into your system in the required amounts on tap. Gambling became your way of feeling good by filling that void within you.

Although society doesn't approve of drug addiction, it is somewhat understood that the addict is hooked on a substance. This substance is something tangible that can be seen which is different from dopamine addiction as this is something you don't go out and buy.

Your own body is your dealer, and it's not on your side.

Although dopamine is released naturally into our bodies as part of how our bodies work, these amounts are not significantly high enough to cause a chemical imbalance and are effective because this natural release does only what it is designed to do.

So, let's take a closer look at what's really going on to establish why you are having such a problem overcoming your addiction and how you got into this mess.

- Something deep down within you is not right - there is an emptiness that needs to be filled.

- Your GAM steps in like a parasite which you then host

- You experience the dopamine rush when you start gambling

- Your GAM encourages you to experience this over and over again

- Your own body releases dopamine into your system in high quantities during gambling

- Your GAM overrides your own decision-making process

Just as slots are progressive, so is your gambling addiction, with the need for more and more dopamine

And the casinos know all this.

They know how vulnerable you are. They know you are not in control. They know they can take advantage of you and do this through clever marketing.

It's a wonder any of us make it out at all!

But how do they set us up for exploitation?

Chapter 4

The Setup

"Unfortunately, with addiction, there's manipulation and deception." - Jeremy Camp

ALL THE MANIPULATIONS HAVE played havoc with our sense of reasoning and our ability to deal with reality. I know you've experienced the exceptions below, and they are so effective because of this experience.

If you've never experienced them, you would not believe them, and if you don't believe them, the casino would not be able to take advantage of you.

But remember, exceptions are just that, exceptions. And these exceptions are all part of the setup.

- We Believe Our Luck Will Turn

- We See an Almost-Win as a Win Coming

- We Believe the Longer We Play on a Machine, the Better Chance We Will Win

- If We Get Free Spins, We Will Get More
- If We Have a Terrible Free Spin, Another One Will Follow Closely
- If We Increase Our Bet, We Can Manipulate the Machine to Payout
- The Result of Every Push of the Button Is Random

We Believe Our Luck Will Turn

We've all been there. We put so much into one machine that it becomes impossible to walk away. We know that if we do, we will miss out on the payout that is due. Our luck will turn if we just keep feeding it. We put our human sense of morality into our gameplay.

We know it's just wrong that the machine keeps on taking and taking. We know it's not fair. It's not right and on some level believe the machine will respond appropriately, just as a human being would in similar circumstances.

But it's not human.

It's only a machine in the casino designed to take your money. It has no sense of right or wrong.

We See an Almost-Win as a Win Coming

When the symbols appear that are almost a winning line, our sense of anticipation and excitement increases. We almost got it. This is a sign the payout is on the way. The machine is preparing itself to display that elusive winning line, and if we continue to press that button, we will win.

We Believe the Longer We Play on a Machine, the Better Chance We Will Win

I used to believe in the law of averages. Everything averages out eventually, so it made sense that if I continued to play on a dead machine, there would come a time when it would turn and turn in a big way.

After all, it could not stay dead. It would average out, and I would be there to get all my money back and more, if I continued to play.

If We Get Free Spins, We Will Get More

Finally, we get those free spins. This is a sure sign the machine is warm or getting hot, so another set of free spins should follow shortly.

However, to experience the next set of free spins, we must continue playing and to do this, we bet all the money we just won in our free spins until we end up with less money than we had before our free spin.

If We Have a Terrible Free Spin, Another One Will Follow Closely

We've all had those waste of time spins. We play and play and wait for those spins. And there they are, the required amount of scatter symbols to activate those free spins. This is exciting. This is what we've been playing for and then, nothing.

What?

So, we continue because we know that particular machine is giving free spins, so the fruitful one must be about to follow.

If We Increase Our Bet, We Can Manipulate the Machine to Payout

We often let our impatience get the better of us. When nothing happens, we feel compelled to take charge, take control and make something happen. This usually means we increase our bets with the hope that this action will somehow change how the machine has been playing and it will start paying out, and of course, our winnings will be much more because of our increased bet.

The Result of Every Push of the Button Is Random

We have been misinformed to believe that the result from every push of the button is random. This means that the subsequent press could generate another winning line even after a win. The casinos are saying there is no such thing as a hot or cold machine because everything is completely random, with every result a possibility.

This is what I used to believe.

However, after years of experience, I stopped believing this. If that were the case, then results should be random, and to me, random meant sometimes good, sometimes not so good.

If this is supposedly true, why are we losing over time?

Today's slot machines are computer programs with excellent graphics and captivating sounds. But they remain computer programs that can be coded to do what it is designed to do. And in the case of a slot machine, it is to keep you playing as long as possible, so it can take as much of your money as possible while entertaining and distracting you from what's really going on.

There's nothing random about that.

Loyalty Programs

Most casinos have customer loyalty programs, which operate on a tier system. Those in the highest tier reap the most rewards, which are based both on attitudinal and behavioral loyalty.

In other words, the more you frequent a particular casino and the more you spend, you progress up the tiers.

Therefore, gambling addicts will participate in these programs to benefit from the rewards that are offered, which often include gaming credits which give you the ability to play for longer.

In research by Hollingshead et al. (2021), "*As a result, some researchers and policy-makers have expressed concern that loyalty programs in the gambling industry fuel excessive gambling, particularly among people living with a gambling disorder who are more likely to enroll in such programs.*"

Additionally, there is a social aspect known as social identity theory, wherein reaching the highest tier of the casino loyalty program will elevate the player's perceived status and increase their self-worth.

As discussed earlier, self-worth or lack thereof can be a contributing factor in the early stages of gambling addiction, so belonging to that special group of people can falsely improve this, making this aspect extremely difficult to walk away from.

> "*The motivation to belong to high status groups may lead casino loyalty members to accelerate their spending as they approach the points needed to achieve a higher tier - an instantiation of goal-gradient hypothesis. Additionally, higher tier players are motivated to maintain a high level of play to avoid being*

> bumped down to a lower status should their play decrease in frequency or spend. Maintaining one's high status requires sustained high-frequency play. Should such play result in the player spending more than they can afford, they may be at risk for developing a gambling disorder." (Hollingshead et al., 2021)

As I've told you before, I was hooked on a particular slot machine which I have referred to as "my" slot machine. Imagine the horror I felt one day when I arrived at the casino to find that whole row of machines switched off. These machines were being converted to play different games. I was beyond upset.

I called the casino office and immediately, two of the Directors invited me for coffee to discuss the problem. I gave them my two cents worth, and they listened to everything I had to say. I felt so important.

Playing back that conversation in my head now is quite embarrassing.

They must have thought I was a crazy person. And at the time, as I was completely immersed in my gambling addiction, they were right.

I told them I understood games got changed, but they gave no warning of this, and I didn't get the chance to enjoy playing on that machine knowing it would be the last time.

It's almost like I didn't get to say goodbye.

They said all the right things and apologized and gave me extra gaming credits. I know they would never have done any of this if I hadn't been in the highest tier of their loyalty program.

These programs are highly effective and play a significant role in contributing to gambling addiction. You are certainly not alone in your problem, as compulsive gamblers contribute greatly to the casinos' revenue.

> "The USA is in the top list of countries, where a large part of the population (2.6% or almost 10 million people) has an addiction problem because of gambling. These activities are represented in every state (even where they are restricted)." (Statistics of Gambling Addiction 2016, n.d.)

And in the UK (*Statistics of Gambling Addiction 2016*, n.d.), "The percentage of people who suffer from the bad influences of gambling varies from 0.6 to 1.1% of the total adult population."

With online gambling, simply opening an account allows you to receive benefits from the casino. This usually begins with being enticed to play at a particular casino where you will receive free money just for opening the account followed by percentage bonuses for the money you deposit. The more funds you deposit, the higher the percentage bonus.

The casinos don't just give away money for nothing. This is all part of a cleverly designed setup to get you hooked to take your money in the long run.

Mixed Messages from Casinos

Casinos are legally required to provide Safer Gambling Programs. Online casinos offer settings where you can limit your deposits and monthly spending. They have hotlines you can call and provide self-exclusion options. They will send automated emails or text messages when you are flagged as a player spending excessively.

This all leads to a feeling of safety. This is just another part of the setup. They don't care about you. This is all about being compliant. Casinos pretend to help with their Safer Gambling Programs. Pretend to care about you while using every trick in the book to manipulate you into spending more money.

I had a telephone call from an online casino representative of their Safer Gambling team to check in on me as they had noticed a higher rate of play in both time and money. Honestly, I thought this was a joke. The person sounded like a teenager who had a written list of questions to ask so they could simply be ticked off. Job done. We checked in.

I told them everything I knew they wanted to hear. The last thing I wanted was for them to impose restrictions on my account. And despite knowing that compulsive gamblers are seldom truthful regarding their addiction, they accepted everything I said as the truth. They did not ask more probing questions. They didn't even ask me to provide proof of income to back up what I was telling them. I was just a name on a list, a task to be ticked off.

And of course, once their job was done, I continued to receive bonuses and rewards and was continually enticed to deposit and spend more.

Casino Design

You don't feel relaxed and excited at the casino without reason. From the minute you arrive, everything you see and hear has been carefully thought out to set you up to make those deposits, and often into specific slot machines.

Some of these tactics include:

- Attractive games with familiar themes

- Flashing lights but laid-back environment

- Electronic credits and printed vouchers so your money is not seen as real money

- Game placement in high-traffic areas

- No clocks or natural lighting so you have no sense of time

- Free drinks, including alcohol

- Rewards and incentives

- Sounds and upbeat music

So, all in all, despite the occasional good wins, I never really won.

Winnings would sometimes counter the losses experienced but never exceed them. Over time, the losses grew, but it's more than just financial losses. It's time and energy, and when you feel down and can't trust your own decisions, you can't get far in your life.

We are all so much more deserving and capable than we might believe, but if we don't take the time to explore our full potential, we will never realize what we can really be or what we could accomplish.

When we get rid of the false plug that we think is filling us up inside, we make room for something real - something sustainable that will bring us joy.

But how did we get ourselves into this situation?

Chapter 5

Did You Inherit Your Gambling Addiction?

*"**Your genetics load the gun.
Your lifestyle pulls the trigger.**"* - Mehmet Oz

I UNDERSTAND THAT SOME people can be preset to addiction and impulsive behavior, however, this should not become an excuse. In fact, if you know this and understand what this means, then steps should be taken to avoid situations that bring about the circumstances that trigger this behavior.

A relative told me a baby story about myself a few years ago. I had never known my birth father, nor know anything about him other than his name. The whole circumstance about my biological father was a bit of a mystery that my mother never talked about and for some reason, I never asked her about either.

Anyway, this relative of mine told me on the day of my christening, she was with me, my mother and father, and some other family members. My mother was getting me ready and doing everything a good mother would do on a special day like this to ensure I looked adorable and that everybody was looked after.

She told me that my father completely ignored me. He was too busy focused on his horse racing as he was a compulsive gambler, addicted to betting on the horses, and had no time for me, my mother, or anything else.

This was one of the reasons that my mother left him when I was less than a year old.

When I heard this story, I was not upset about being ignored as I did not know this man. Instead, as I have never known him or anything about him, I found it interesting that he was a compulsive gambler.

Somehow it seemed that although we weren't connected, we had something in common. I wondered whether this contributed genetically to my own slots gambling addiction and decided to investigate this more.

Is Gambling in Your Genes?

Genes are passed from parents to children. The information contained within these genes determines our characteristics and physicality. If you have blue eyes or brown hair, this information would be contained in the genes you inherited at conception.

You will get half your genes from your mother and half from your father, making you a unique individual. Even when you have siblings, you will still be unique because the mix of genes you receive from both parents is random.

These genes are made up of sequences of DNA in the chromosomes in the cell nucleus, where they are specifically arranged. They contain instructions for the manufacturing of specific proteins which then determine your physical characteristics and traits.

It's easy to understand then why you look the way you do. However, our genes also determine other factors that cannot be seen, including predisposition to certain illnesses or brain functionality.

Our genes will determine whether we are more likely to be obese, suffer cancer, or experience other mental disorders. And just as our genes can determine these negative characteristics, we can also inherit genes that positively impact us, like math skills or talents.

In other words, we can inherit genes that make us susceptible to pathological gambling.

"By looking into the molecular genetics of gambling addiction, the study identified specific forms of genes — known as allele variants — that directly correspond with the chemical messengers associated with pathological gambling. The link between these chemical messengers and pathological gambling suggests that certain people may be more genetically inclined to become addicted to gambling due to how their brains interact with the happy hormones and positive feelings that gambling can often produce." (Is Gambling Hereditary, n.d.)

Just because our body contains genes that mean we are more likely to become a compulsive gambler than somebody who doesn't have that gene doesn't mean that we will become a pathological gambler. It only means that in certain circumstances, these chemical messengers can be triggered, and we will find ourselves on the path of addiction.

Even if we go to the casino and gamble for a few hours, and even if we have this gene, this doesn't mean we will become addicted. It's more complex than this, and other factors in our life have a role to play.

As humans, we need to feel happy. Dopamine is known as the happy hormone. When we experience positive relationships, are in love, achieve goals or overcome challenges, we feel happiness. Our hormones are in harmony, and our brains interact normally with the happy hormones.

Unfortunately, if there is an emptiness within you, looking to be filled, the excitement you feel at the casino can trigger your brain to release dopamine. As there seems to be nothing else to latch onto, your brain will begin associating gambling with happiness.

Still, that happiness is overshadowed by other factors that leave you feeling empty or detached. You may say that doesn't make sense because you are happily married, have beautiful children, or have a successful career, so you get happiness elsewhere. And you would be partly right. However, on some level within you, your brain has not been interpreting this correctly, or one area is not so great.

The highs you experience when gambling are instant and long-lasting. With every bet placed or push of the button, your senses are heightened, your heart will race, and you feel that anything is possible.

When you are not really experiencing these feelings in your day-to-day life, you become addicted to the experience that will give you this feeling, like gambling. And you want to enjoy this as much and as often as possible.

Gambling is only the facilitator. You become addicted to the thrill but believe you are happy. And even when you realize you have a problem and want to quit, your brain seems to loop the original message that gambling makes you happy.

According to (Eisen et al., 1998), "*familial factors have an important influence on risk for pathological gambling behavior. The increasing access to legalized gambling is likely to result in a higher prevalence of pathological gambling behavior among individuals who are more vulnerable because of familial factors.*"

Although you received the genes from your parents that predispose you to gambling addiction, you cannot blame them for this because you created the environment that allowed your GAM to take control.

As an emotional being, you simply wanted to feel positive emotions and were lured into the trap of thinking gambling was the answer. This differs from genes that ensure you have blue eyes as you have no control over that.

And although you didn't understand that your genetics would influence your behavior at the time, now you do.

My Something Else

I understand that genetics was not the sole reason for my gambling but played a role in my own brain makeup with low impulse control. This fact, coupled with something else, created my own GAM.

So, what was that something else?

It will be different for everybody, but from my experience and everything I have learned, I believe it comes down to something missing in your life. There is an emptiness deep inside that needs to be filled. This was not a conscious thought but something I have been able to see with hindsight.

Betrayal has been a constant theme in my life.

Obviously, this started with being abandoned by my father to being abandoned by my mother's second husband, my adoptive father, and many other abandonment experiences.

This all contributed to my own feelings of insecurity, and I didn't really talk about these things. Of course, I had so many wonderful life experiences too, but somehow none of these impacted me in the way they should have because the void was too deep.

I always felt something was missing but could never quite put my finger on it. It was only in my later years that I understood what the problem had been all along, as I began to get a grip on my compulsion, and this was part of the process.

And I was only able to finally figure this out completely when gambling was no longer my priority.

I also learned that until we confront and deal with our problems, they will keep showing up one way or another, so if we don't want to continue to live in the shadow of our past, the sooner we face our problems, the better off we will be.

As long as you are gambling, that void will be filled by your GAM, and you will never experience the wholeness you long for. While gambling may have been a great solution and distraction initially, you probably feel more isolated and emptier than ever before.

Addiction vs. Pastime

Addiction is different from a pastime in that addiction compels you to engage in an activity at every opportunity, whereas a pastime is something you enjoy doing in your free time.

A pastime is not something that is prioritized above everything else and does not impact your sense of self or finances negatively. Usually, a pastime will benefit you in some way and is often referred to as a hobby. As the word implies, this is something you do to pass the time.

- You Improve or Acquire a Skill
- Money Is Not Wasted
- You Have Something to Show for It
- You Are Happy to Discuss with Others
- Makes You Feel Worthwhile

You Improve or Acquire a Skill

Hobbies generally include things that allow you to develop your skill set further. This could be taking up a sport like tennis, fishing or surfing, learning to bake and decorate cakes, knitting or crocheting, or photography or writing. The possibilities are endless. Every time you take part in it, you will improve.

Money Is Not Wasted

Although most hobbies will require some financial investment, the money is not wasted if you are actively involved in that activity.

Tennis rackets, surfboards, and cake tins all cost money but are essential to enjoy that particular pastime. You will also not risk your sanity by buying a tennis racket or a few balls of wool.

You Have Something to Show for It

Your pastime will produce positive results, whether they are tangible or not. You will win more tennis matches, make delicious and beautifully decorated cakes or take great pictures that tell a story.

There is definite progress from where you started out that can be seen.

You are Happy to Discuss with Others

There is no shame in discussing your hobby. You take pleasure in telling others what you are doing and what you've achieved.

You will share these experiences by showing your pictures or giving them cake, and most people who know you well, will be well aware of what you enjoy doing and how good you are at it.

Makes You Feel Worthwhile

As you improve in your abilities, you will feel genuine confidence and pride in yourself which does wonders for your self-esteem and can positively impact other areas of your life.

And if gambling is something you enjoy every now and then, just as you would a visit to the beach, cinema, park, or museum, and is not impacted by any other statements below, then I don't think you have anything to worry about even if you have the gambling gene.

How to Recognize You Have a Gambling Problem

If your feelings about gambling today differ from when you first started and include any of the following points, you are more likely to have a gambling problem. The more points you relate to from the following list, the more pathological your addiction will be.

- Gambling Is Always on Your Mind
- Increasing Bets
- Chasing Losses
- Needing to Gamble
- Irritability and Moodiness
- Borrowing Money
- Being Deceitful

Gambling Is Always on Your Mind

When you're gambling, that's all you're thinking about. You're not thinking about your to-do list, what your family or friends will think, your job, and especially not your finances in the healthy way you should. If your finances are on your mind, you're probably only thinking about how much more money you have available to spend on gambling.

Increasing Bets

To maintain or increase that high, your bets are increased so that the reward if you hit it big will be higher. Of course, the downside of this is that you will be losing more at an increasingly unsustainable rate. You know this, yet you continue to spend more regardless.

Chasing Losses

When you've lost money, you feel compelled to continue depositing money as you feel this is the only way you have to recoup the money you've already spent. This is done against your better judgment, where you know that you are throwing good money after bad but are unable to stop yourself.

Needing to Gamble

When the urge to gamble strikes, it's overwhelming. It's more than just a thought of doing something. Your brain races into gear to make it happen regardless of whether it's a good idea that can be afforded or whether you originally had other plans. When you want to gamble, that's all you focus on. You want to just gamble.

Irritability and Moodiness

Sometimes you just can't give in to those urges due to prior commitments. You may be at work or home with the children or at a friend's house for dinner, so you can't just get up and go.

Being confined with no control over the situation makes you irritable and moody, which can only be relieved when you enter the casino.

Borrowing Money

You find you have to borrow money to gamble. This can be before a gambling session to have money to gamble, or afterward to replace the money you lost, so you have money to live on until you receive your next paycheck.

Being Deceitful

You are not entirely honest with yourself about your gambling or honest with others. You often have secretive casino visits when you can to keep the extent of your gambling habit hidden and to avoid the inevitable questions that force you to lie.

Being Susceptible to Addiction

Remember being susceptible to gambling doesn't mean you are only vulnerable to that. You are predisposed to become addicted to anything that can put your hormones out of whack.

Anything that begins to have more control over you than you have over it has the potential to turn into an addiction.

The last thing you want to do, or need in your life, is to substitute one addiction for another. It may be fantastic to finally free yourself from your gambling addiction, but if you haven't dealt with the root causes of your problem, you will find you still have a void that needs to be filled and it could be very easy to just swap one addiction for another.

Now that you have a clearer understanding regarding the role of genetics in your addiction, it's time to explore what your something else could possibly be, so that you can finally be completely free of your gambling addiction, without the possibility of getting trapped in another detrimental behavioral addiction.

Chapter 6

Evaluate Your GAM

> *"If you know the enemy and know yourself, you need not fear the result of a hundred battles. If you know yourself but not the enemy, for every victory gained you will also suffer a defeat. If you know neither the enemy nor yourself, you will succumb in every battle."*
> - Sun Tzu, The Art of War

IT'S TIME TO GET to know your enemy.

Although it may feel like it, you are not your enemy. I know you blame yourself for your behavior and the damage this has caused. You are right to feel some responsibility, but I don't want you to carry that burden of guilt anymore.

With the discovery of your GAM, you now have a better understanding of what's been going on within you all this time. You have been the host to a monster that has controlled and manipulated you, who overrode your own power of reasoning and lured you down a path of self-destruction.

However, you mustn't use this as an excuse. This is not a get-out-of-jail-free card where you can simply excuse your behavior and consequences.

You are still part of the problem.

Your Role in the Problem

While evaluating your GAM and its role in your addiction, it is first necessary to explore your own role in this regard.

"If one of the partners in an association is much larger than the other, it is generally known as the host. In parasitism, the parasite benefits at the host's expense." - (Wikipedia Host (biology), 2022)

As the larger partner in this host-parasite relationship, you have played the role of host.

The same Wikipedia page goes on to explain that *"some organisms live in close association with a host and only become parasitic when environmental conditions deteriorate."* (Wikipedia Host (biology), 2022)

Although this Wikipedia page explains physical parasites in biology, using these examples allows a picture to be painted which is easier to understand.

There's a strong probability that your GAM has been lying dormant within you for many years, just waiting for the right conditions in your life to occur to make itself known. During this dormant phase, you had no knowledge of its existence.

A simple visit to the casino would not be considered the right circumstance. Millions of people all over the world gamble for fun occasionally and are never subjected to the cravings of the GAM.

So, what is the right circumstance?

This will be different for everybody, but fundamentally the host feels empty inside. Something is missing. This is the void that the GAM enters and fills. Your feeling of emptiness dissipates with each spin of the reels, and life takes on a new meaning.

Only you know what void your GAM is filling, and we'll explore this more in a later chapter.

How Did Your GAM Take Control?

Although the simple answer to this question is that you gave it the power to control you, it's more complicated than that.

Nobody willingly gives up control. Nobody wants to be controlled. It's more often the case that the addicted gambler feels that they have no control over their lives at all, and instead of facing their problems and dealing with them, their gambling addiction subconsciously becomes their focus for this lack of control.

This occurs because dealing with the real cause of the feeling of lack of control is too painful or difficult.

With the real problem underlying the addiction not being dealt with, no relief is experienced. However, by transferring this pain to the GAM, there are very powerful moments of relief.

In these moments, reality is forgotten, and you can enjoy moments of "normality", where you are no longer feeling emotional pain.

Of course, this is only how it starts. Compulsive gambling becomes another emotional pain point, leaving you doubly afflicted, trapped, and overwhelmed.

But in the early stages of your addiction, the stress you feel now was only fleeting. Although you may not have enjoyed losing, you were not in the hole you are in today.

Clarity

I refer to those times between gambling sessions, when your GAM is dormant, as moments of clarity. In these moments, we are not under the control of our GAM. We can think clearly. We are calm. Apart from the stress we may have caused ourselves by losing too much money, we are at peace. And once we are over the guilt of our last gambling session, we are determined never to let that happen again.

This is how you will feel all the time when you stop gambling, but even better. As you will no longer be throwing your money away, your financial stress will lighten, and you will no longer feel those awful emotions of guilt and shame.

When your GAM appears, this feeling is replaced with that uncontrollable urge to gamble. The internal battle commences because you know you shouldn't, but you feel powerless to resist your GAM. You want this battle to be over. You want to feel good again and so once again, you give in and do what you always do.

You do this because this is how you eventually get back to the feeling of clarity.

Gambling is the vehicle that takes you there. This is what your brain tells you. You listen to your GAM so you can feel good again.

Clarity is where you want to be, all the time. Where you are not influenced. Where your decisions are your own. Where you feel your life has possibilities. Where you have no GAM.

So, what if you could find another vehicle to get you there?

Your Dis-Ease

What I mean by using the word dis-ease, is that you are not at ease. Something is wrong, which can lead to actual disease or mental disorders.

Problem gambling is classified as a gambling disorder which is a behavioral addiction diagnosis.

> "*Substance-Related and Addictive Disorders. People with these diagnoses have problems associated with excessive use of alcohol, opioids (for example, oxycodone and morphine), recreational drugs, hallucinogens, and six other types of drugs. This group also includes gambling disorder.*" (Salters-Pedneault, PhD, 2021)

We know our gambling addiction has a medical classification that can be treated just as other behavioral addictions.

Your gambling disorder didn't appear out of nowhere. As previously mentioned, you possibly could have inherited the predisposition to gambling, but still, something would have triggered that.

Your GAM knows exactly what buttons to push (pun intended) to get you to do its bidding. The buttons your GAM pushes will be different from the buttons mine pushed because your fundamental issues will be different from mine.

So how did your GAM get this information? How does it know how to manipulate you?

As you know, your GAM is not you. It only lives within you and feeds off you.

And because it resides within you, it has access to what is within you, often deep down within you, those thoughts you don't like to think about, those emotions you don't want to feel which you have buried. Its hooks go deep.

It looks for your dis-ease.

Once it's found your dis-ease, it turns your own pain against you. But it's oh so clever and oh so subtle that you don't even realize it's happening.

In actuality, what is occurring is that your GAM taps into your hidden pain, and learns how to manipulate you, provides you with temporary relief from your deep pain, but causes you additional pain in the process.

So now you have double pain.

But the relief you experience from the hidden pain is so good that you can easily cope with the second pain you are now experiencing from your gambling addiction. The pain you feel from your addiction is far easier to carry than your original, hidden pain.

And that's why you keep gambling. That's how you became addicted.

You simply want the hidden pain to end, and your gambling addiction and the consequential pain of it is far less painful than that pain.

And in those moments of clarity, between your gambling sessions, you aren't experiencing any pain at all.

Your root pain, your dis-ease is buried deep, and you are not dealing with it or facing it. The calm you feel replaces the pain associated with your gambling, and you enjoy that. You hold onto that, focus on that, and for a short time, you feel almost normal.

But your GAM hasn't gone away. It's been lying dormant, waiting for the right opportunity to pounce, to catch you unawares and pull you back.

Your GAM is attached to your root pain.

To remove your GAM permanently, you must remove the roots; the only way to do this is to dig deep.

Face Your Fear

If only it were that simple. There is a reason why you have avoided dealing with your gambling addiction recovery for so long. Sure, you may have tried before but were unsuccessful.

This was my own experience. And I understand why my recovery attempts were in vain.

Gambling is the plaster that covers your dis-ease. When you focus only on the plaster and not the dis-ease underneath, your progress will be slow or will not occur at all, and you will continue to cycle through gambling and recovery.

The only way to ensure long-lasting success is to finally face your fears and deal with the root problem. For far too long, you've been avoiding this, perhaps believing that if you don't think about it, it will go away, or you simply learn to live with it.

Well, how's that been working out for you?

Maybe you've been afraid of what you'll find, or perhaps you're worried that you will still feel empty and incomplete even if you deal with it.

Unless you are happy as you are now with your gambling addiction, there is no choice but to move past the fear and confront whatever needs to be dealt with.

You have avoided this for far too long. You now have the opportunity for real growth and happiness in your life.

I think you know it. It's time to dig deep.

Spiritual Awakening

I have mentioned before that part of my recovery involved getting back in touch with my spiritual side. As we are all unique, this will mean different things to each of us, but for me, it meant connecting with my inner being. This is my eternal being, not the physical body having this life experience.

Proper recovery from any addiction needs a holistic approach. This means you must focus on your body, mind, and spirit. Your body needs to be well nourished, fit, and rested. Your mind needs to be clear, calm, and open to new suggestions and learning opportunities. Your spirit is the glue that holds everything together in perfect harmony when you are in tune with it.

Although I hadn't been focused on improving all three, my spiritual side was the part of myself that I had ignored for far too long. I was occupied with the outer world and constantly looked for ways to feel better, confident and loved.

Of course, this was the entirely wrong approach, which did not serve me well or provide me with the solutions, insight, or understanding I needed.

By focusing on my spiritual side, I was able to tap into a different energy, and that energy enabled me to find the courage and strength to go beyond the thoughts that had been limiting me.

As my knowledge and understanding grew, I began to feel lighter even though I was still gambling, although not as much at this time. There was an undeniable shift in how I felt and my perspective.

Let me give you something to think about.

I don't mean to be corny here by quoting a few expressions below, but they helped me when I thought about them.

You may have heard the expression, *if you fail to go within, you go without,* and it's so relevant here.

Going Without

When you go without, you deprive yourself of something you could have, but you learn to live without it. And when you don't have something after a while, you don't even miss it or realize it's missing.

It also means that you search for what you need externally, and in the case of the addicted gambler, this is in the casino.

Going Within

When you go within, you look inside yourself for two reasons. Firstly, that is the essence of you, and this is what you need to do to get back on the path to being your true self.

And secondly, this is where your GAM resides, with its roots firmly planted in your dis-ease.

So, you can see the importance of going within. That is where the magic happens, not at the casino.

According to Kumar(n.d.), "*The universal law, "As within, so without," puts it more succinctly. That is why our spiritual teachers say that the key to eliminating something from our external world is to eliminate it from our internal world of thought and feeling. It is well said that there is no reality outside of the mind. Everything we perceive in the world has its roots in our inner world of thoughts, feelings, and beliefs.*"

Your Outer World Is a Reflection of Your Inner World

This one hit home because I had been looking at my problems from the wrong perspective. I had thought that because my life was in turmoil this was causing me stress and feelings of guilt and shame.

My dis-ease was buried within and was freely available for my GAM to get stuck to. Although I was not actively thinking about my deep issues, I thought I was fine, but just because I wasn't thinking about them, they were still there, deep within me, causing me pain.

I thought I was avoiding these issues successfully. I thought they were behind me. I falsely believed that my unhappiness and feelings of unworthiness resulted from my gambling addiction and self-destructive behavior.

But in truth, it works the other way around.

When I understood this concept, I was motivated and encouraged to explore my issues and resolve my problems from the inside out instead of the outside in.

> *"We do not see things as they are. We see things as we are."* Rabbi Shemuel ben Nachmani, (55b.)

If we wish our lives to be different, we need to be different. It is ourselves that have had the power all along.

Another important thing I learned was that everything that was meant for me would come to me. I had to stop chasing things I thought I wanted, and this included big casino wins. If it was meant for me, it would happen, and I could somehow relate to this because the most significant wins I'd ever experienced had come out of the blue. The incredible losses were when I chased after the win and fought with the slot machine.

But this applies to life in general. Get your house in order. Learn what you can. Focus on your health, mental attitude, and your relationships. Work hard at something you enjoy, so you can thrive and not just survive and let your spirit guide you. Learn to trust your own judgment again and follow your intuition.

This is the goal to be free and happy and you need to put real effort into getting there.

And I know you can because the alternative is devastating.

Chapter 7

Betting Your Life Away

"By gaming, we lose both our time and treasure, two things most precious to the life of man."
- Owen Feltham

I KNOW WHILE YOU'RE gambling at the casino, suicide is the last thing on your mind, but do you realize that every push of the button has the potential to bring the possibility of suicide to you?

And with every push of that button, this day is coming closer.

No matter what treatment you opt for, whether through counseling or an organization such as Gambler's Anonymous or even the self-help option, nothing will work unless you have a <u>fundamental desire to recover</u>.

With that desire, anything is possible. But, of course, this requires change.

You Will Definitely Stop Gambling

You will stop gambling one way or another.

1. Hitting Rock Bottom

2. Death by Suicide

3. Making a Conscious Decision

Hitting Rock Bottom

How will you feel when you have lost everything? You'll have nothing left. Your finances, many of your relationships, maybe even your job, your car, and your home will be gone. You'll eventually be left with a pile of debts and a self-image even lower than the one you had before you became addicted.

This is where your GAM is leading you.

This is rock bottom. The only positive thing about hitting rock bottom is your GAM will leave you. You will no longer be gambling. Instead of dealing with the internal conflict you used to experience before, you will be left with overwhelming regret.

You will admonish yourself for not seeing the writing on the wall and for not acting and doing something about the problem while you still had the chance.

And today is the day you still have that chance!

When you hit rock bottom, your secret will be out. You will feel the judgment from others. You will feel shame. You will have no resources of your own and will become dependent upon the generosity of others. And although these others are helping you, they are usually the same others that are judging you.

As much as they want to understand, they don't. Not really. How could they? After all, *you* don't even understand how you could have been so foolish. How could you have thrown everything away with the simple press of a button?

Of course, there was never anything simple about pressing that button and by now hopefully, you have some insight into what has been going on inside you. Hopefully, something has shifted within you to motivate you to make that change while you still have the choice to do so, before you hit rock bottom and your choices and options are gone.

I don't want you to hit rock bottom and believe me, you don't want to be there either. And if you don't want to be there, what are you doing to do about it?

Death by Suicide

According to new research (Samaritans New Guidelines Equip Gambling Businesses to Do More to Prevent Suicide, 2021), *"Research has found a clear association between gambling and suicide. People experiencing gambling-related harms are more likely to experience suicidal thoughts and suicide attempts than the general population."*

Although this information is shocking, it is not surprising. With everything seemingly stacked against the addicted gambler, many feel this is the only way out.

Living without the ability to trust yourself, low self-worth, financial difficulty, guilt, and shame are all contributing factors. Not being able to talk freely without judgment from society makes this one of the most complex and most misunderstood afflictions.

Constantly feeling under pressure to gamble. Continually feeling the stress of financial manipulation and always living with the burden of guilt and shame is often just too much to bear.

Unfortunately, many addicted gamblers have tried to stop before but often relapse and feel that they will never be able to recover.

And sadly, for many, suicide looks like the only way out.

However, relapsing should be seen as part of the process. This is in no way, shape or form indicative that you will not be able to recover and move on to live a happy and healthy life.

> *"Whatever recovery path they choose, about 90% of problem gamblers relapse, a slightly higher rate than for other types of addicts. This doesn't mean recovery is near impossible to achieve, says Hodgins, but indicates that addicts often make several attempts before they succeed."* (Collier, 2008)

I also experienced relapse during my recovery journey, and it's essential to see this as a journey with highs and lows, which will get easier as you continue. Your journey will be unique to you with the common destination of recovery.

If you use the strength you have displayed throughout your gambling addiction, you will finally reach, what may seem at this time, that elusive destination of finally slaying your GAM and putting your gambling into a past chapter of your life.

I understand that there is the possibility that you may be severely depressed and are experiencing suicidal thoughts. I want you to believe that help is at hand, to not only recover, but to go on and live a fulfilling life that may seem quite impossible to you today.

Making a Conscious Decision

You will stop gambling. That day will come. It doesn't have to be because you hit rock bottom; it shouldn't be by suicide.

If you genuinely want to get control back, live authentically, and build a life you can be proud of, where you feel inner peace and happiness, your only choice is to make the conscious decision to stop gambling.

Now.

You need to stop gambling while you still have choices. You want to stop gambling before you've lost everything while you still have the ability to turn your life around to focus on your financial stability and relationships, and more importantly, yourself.

If you're afraid of what a gambling-free future looks like and are scared to commit to it, just imagine what a gambling-free future will look like when this is forced upon you because you simply don't have the funds to gamble anymore.

You won't even have the funds to live a normal life where you are in control. You will be controlled by others, thereby trading the control of your GAM to control by other people.

And they will control you.

They will have expectations from you, and if you want their help, you will have no choice but to live up to their expectations.

Wouldn't it be far wiser to have expectations of yourself and live up to them? Not only is this wiser, but it's also easier.

You have the power to implement the changes and put in place the steps that will serve you best, not what other people think is best for you.

The last thing you want is to find yourself trapped in another situation that you created, a situation that will be far more difficult to remove yourself from than the situation you are in today.

The only thing that may prevent you from making this decision is if you are still under the illusion that you can come out of this intact if you continue to gamble in that you will be different from everybody else. You will not lose everything.

And you may be right. You may not lose everything, but haven't you lost enough already? I don't know you, but I do know what you've already lost. And it's all so pointless and unnecessary.

Isn't now the time to invest in yourself and your recovery?

Isn't it time for action?

Chapter 8

Time for Action

"Recovery is not for people who need it. It's for people who want it." - Unknown

YOU WANT YOUR RECOVERY to be real and lasting; to accomplish that, it's important to be realistic.

Let's get real.

Dig Deep

I know this will probably be one of the hardest things you have ever done in your life, but I promise you, the life you want and the person you want to be is there waiting for you.

Before you make inroads with your addiction, you need to dig deep and go within to find the source of your dis-ease. You may be able to do this on your own, as I did, or you may need the help of a therapist.

I don't suggest that this is going to be easy.

Only you will know what will work for you, and it's up to you to decide what that is and take the necessary steps to establish, confront and heal from whatever has been holding you back from being the wonderful and happy woman you are meant to be.

Anyway, after years of gambling, I finally realized enough was enough. This was not an overnight decision but a gradual realization of what had been going on with me.

Although I have always believed that I am a special soul, as we all are, I had neglected this part of me. With this realization, I became more in touch with my spiritual side. I kept on telling myself that I chose to be here. I was not an accident of pro-creation. I am more than my body.

By focusing on my spiritual side, rather than my mental or physical, I felt more in tune with myself and consequently more in control.

I realized the behavior I had been practicing was reflecting how I felt treated by the world. I felt betrayed and had trust issues, and by my compulsive gambling, I was mirroring that action by betraying myself, the real me, the spiritual me, which meant I could not even trust myself.

In simple terms, over time, my attitude changed, and so my behavior changed. As stated, this did not happen overnight. I did not stop gambling immediately, but as I began to ask myself the hard questions and spent time looking deep within to find the answers, a shift occurred within me until I no longer felt compelled to gamble.

Before finally sorting myself out, I had tried other things to stop without success. After a particularly bad online gambling session, where I had even used funds on my husband's credit card, I joined the UK Gamblers Program and self-excluded myself from casinos for six months.

I am sure this program has helped many people, but it did not work for me. I must be honest in stating that I did not complete the program because, after about three sessions on the phone with a counselor, I did not feel she would be able to help me.

Firstly, she had a strong accent that prevented me from understanding everything she said without asking her to keep repeating it, which did not make for a good flow of conversation. I know I could probably have asked for somebody else, but I didn't.

In these conversations, I just felt it was about money. Did I not understand that I was never going to win? Of course, I knew that, so she wasn't telling me anything I didn't already know. She was not reaching me as an individual with specific triggers or issues.

Of course, the six-month self-exclusion program worked where I could not gamble. All my online casino accounts were locked, and land-based casinos are not a big thing in the UK. There aren't many of them; they are very small and don't have the slots I like to play, and of course, being self-excluded meant I legally couldn't gamble there either.

This was an excellent thing.

During those six months, I felt free. I didn't miss it. No GAM was talking me into gambling. I was content and could focus on other things, which I did. I felt happier than I had in a long time, and I improved my financial situation.

However, once those six months were up, I decided to log in again just for fun, after all, I knew I didn't have to gamble all the time as I had been perfectly fine for the six months I hadn't.

However, this was not the case. The GAM was instantly back. "You deserve to spend money on yourself doing what you enjoy". I told myself that I hadn't spent any money gambling in six months, etc. I won't get hooked again as I have proven that I didn't need to gamble for six months!

And so back I was hooked again. But thankfully, this time was short-lived.

During those six months, I was happy. I had learned new skills and taken on projects I had been afraid of. This may sound silly, but I was intimidated by Instagram, especially for business use, but I did it. I found out everything I could, created an account, wrote over 100 original posts, and got over 3000 followers in less than a year. Now to some of you, this might not be a lot, but to me, it was a tremendous personal achievement.

As I wrote my inspirational Instagram posts, I fed my brain with what I needed to hear. Although I was writing them for others, I realized I was writing them for myself. It was at this time that I finally quit gambling.

After a year of doing Instagram, I realized I did not want to do it anymore. The motivation I had initially felt had gone, and I had achieved what I set out to do. The time I spent with no monetary reward began to feel like I had replaced one addictive behavior for another, and so just like that, I gave it up. But this time, I walked away with pride and more confidence in myself and my abilities.

I also spent time writing to myself from the point of view of my future self. I would tell myself everything I needed to hear, the things nobody else was telling me. This was extremely powerful as I could focus on what a gambling-free future could look like, and the more I wrote, the more I connected with the gambling-free me.

When I finally stopped gambling, I didn't miss it. I had previously been afraid of what the unknown life without gambling would look like, but I needn't have worried. Because the effort I put in before my final gambling session had already paved the path so that I was ready to walk down it towards the life I envisioned for myself.

That new gambling-free life became my focus.

Now my focus is entirely on me. I started selling low-content books on Amazon last year and love the creative side of this, and although I have not had great financial success with this, the joy I feel when someone buys something I created is absolute. I so enjoy learning and growing as a person.

I am now doing a course focusing on writing and selling high-content books, hence why I am here with you today. Even though Gambling Addiction probably isn't the most lucrative topic, there is a demand for it and a clear need, and I knew I had something of value to say.

I didn't see any books primarily focused on women and slots; most had covers that I did not relate to. I thought this was something I could do. I could bring my personal experience to gambling addiction recovery (allocating my years of compulsive gambling to research...lol), and if I could reach one person only and help them, then that would be an achievement.

You have your own reasons for gambling, whether you are aware of them or not. These reasons need to be explored. You need to feel a sense of inner purpose.

Some people will be helped overnight, others will take longer, gradually weaning off as I did. Some might find one practical tip helpful, others may need a combination.

However, the main thing here is that I don't want you to feel guilty if you don't quit immediately. I don't want you to add to your guilt or make you feel like you have failed.

I truly believe that if you really, really, really want to stop, to get rid of your GAM permanently, then this book will provide you with what you need to get on the right path.

I want you to feel encouraged because there is no bigger high than knowing that you have stared your GAM in the face and finally slain it, so you can enjoy inner peace and put your thoughts, time, energy, and money into something of real value to you, for you.

Let's get started.

Stop Getting Played

As previously mentioned, you have been manipulated twice by your GAM and the casino.

Nobody wants to be manipulated, and certainly not on two fronts.

However, for the manipulation to be successful, you must be a willing participant. As long as you were unaware of what was going on, you can be forgiven for allowing this to happen to you. But once you are wise to the situation, it's a different story.

I want you to stop getting played.

To be able to achieve this, you have to take back control. You have to realize that enough is enough so that you can take the first step toward your recovery, to finally be able to live your life as a winner in a way that has nothing to do with gambling.

Discovering what ails you and finally dealing with it allows you to experience the inner peace you have been craving but from a healthier and clearer perspective.

Once you are on the right path, you will be able to successfully redirect your desire to win. Not the same type of win you experience when you are gambling but winning in the sense of believing in yourself and your abilities. Knowing that you are good enough and worthy of living the life you always dreamed for yourself.

It's time to start betting on yourself.

Harness Your Anger

You have a right to feel angry. Be angry at the casinos and how they have set you up and manipulated you. Be angry at your GAM and even angry at yourself for being taken advantage of for so long.

Being angry is one thing but doing something about it is quite another.

Anger can be a healthy emotion if expressed correctly.

"If you're ever in a situation where someone is making you feel that your anger is "wrong" or "bad," remember that it is perfectly healthy to experience anger. Use the feeling as a prompt to look inwards and explore what you need. Developing the skills to cope with anger in

a way that is assertive (rather than suppressing it or lashing out) is the key to not letting the emotion overcome and control you." (Wiley, 2020)

You need to harness your anger and use it productively to make necessary changes. Use this emotion to fuel your energy and commitment to change to ensure you will never be manipulated again.

First Steps First

Before I outline practical steps that you should take to start your recovery, I feel it's important to summarize some of the points I have already discussed to have an overview of what's coming next and the actions you need to take.

Recognition and Understanding

It's time to recognize what has been going on and the reality of the situation you have been in so that you are no longer manipulated or tricked by the thoughts that your GAM sends you.

Your GAM thoughts are caused by a chemical imbalance in your brain causing you to be a compulsive gambler. You are not your thoughts. With this understanding, you can start to do something about it.

Acceptance

It's time to accept the hard truth of your reality. Not only is it pointless to be in denial about your gambling compulsion, but it's also counter-productive to your recovery. Recovery from your addiction is your goal, the result you are working towards. And as all journeys have a starting point, you need one too.

Your starting point is to accept you are a compulsive gambler.

This doesn't mean you have to beat yourself up about it. On the contrary, this is a positive step and should be treated as such. Just as you would show compassion for somebody else with a problem, it's time to show that same compassion to yourself.

This doesn't mean you are giving yourself a free pass but instead releasing yourself from the burden of guilt and shame that you have carried for so long.

To move forward successfully, you need to be in the right frame of mind. Negative thoughts and emotions will not only hinder your progress but will keep you in that self-destructive cycle.

You want to break free from that cycle and in order to do so, you need to break free from those same thoughts that got you and kept you there.

Accept what you've done. Be kind and forgive yourself. Release the guilt. Release the shame.

Purposeful Focus

It's time to focus on yourself. Focus on more constructive behaviors and rewire your brain. A problem can't be solved from the same mindset, perspective, and attitude that created it.

Solutions are found from a fresh point of view. You need to adopt a can-do attitude and work hard to change the way you think.

Practical Steps

So, you've come this far in the book and probably have lots of thoughts and may be uncertain of what to do next, how to start, or even where to start.

The first thing is to make the conscious decision that you want to stop gambling.

Unless you make this decision for yourself, for your future, everything else you do will not be effective and you will only be dabbling with the idea of recovery.

There are things you can do immediately and then things you can do on an ongoing basis until your GAM is in your rearview mirror and you feel better within and about yourself, more than you've felt in years.

TODAY

- Finish Reading This Book
- Download the Pre Gambling Questions
- Write a Personal Mission Statement

TOMORROW

- Block Online Gambling Sites
- Block Gambling Transactions in Your Banking App
- Join a Self-Exclusion Program

ONGOING

- Connect with Your Spiritual Side
- Write Letters from Your Future Self
- Take a Holistic Approach
- Work on Your Finances

Finish Reading This Book

Finish reading this book today and if you haven't already done so, I suggest you also download my free e-book *Fear of Gambling Addiction Recovery* which may also provide extra insight and motivation.

Download the Pre Gambling Questions

Although it is my sincere hope that you will decide to stop gambling immediately, I know not everyone is going to instantly stop gambling today. If this is you, please don't feel guilty about this as you probably have a lot of work to do on yourself first, so that you can be in the right frame of mind and recover permanently without relapsing. Also, don't use this understanding as a green light to simply continue on as before.

If you've made the decision to stop, then you need to begin doing things differently from today in order to start to break the patterns that have got you into this situation.

Please commit today to completing the Pre Gambling Questions before you gamble again. This in itself, is a giant step towards your recovery as you will, at the very least, be breaking the typical habit by adding a preventive and revealing step.

See this as a block you have to overcome before gambling. More often than not, the mere act of facing the questions and becoming conscious of the answers, will prevent you from actual gambling. Are you answering or is it your GAM?

Most compulsive gamblers don't give much thought prior to a gambling session.

They feel compelled to gamble and just do so.

Some Questions Include:

What is happening right now that you want to gamble? Can you afford to lose the money?

Does gambling today move you closer to YOUR goals or further away?

Knowing that you are putting everything at risk, do YOU really think this is a good idea?

Is there something else you could enjoy with the money that you will lose today?

Is there something else you could enjoy with the time you have right now?

Is this intended gambling session a secretive session? If yes, why? Are these YOUR answers, or your GAM's?

Can you wait an hour before starting a gambling session? Do you have a budget?

To Be Completed the Next Day:

Did you go ahead and gamble or not?

If so, how long did you spend and how much did you lose? If not, what is YOUR main reason for not doing so?

Write a Personal Mission Statement

If living a gambling-free life is your mission, then you need to put this on paper. The act of writing your mission statement will force you to be precise about your goals and the why behind them.

Start off each morning by reading it out loud and reflecting on your words every night before you go to bed. Once done, make copies and place them wherever you can easily see them so that you are constantly reminded of what's important to you.

> "A personal mission statement is much like a corporate mission statement: it describes your convictions, what you stand for, and how you plan to create a life that embodies your values. In other words, it becomes your personal definition of success-one that is separate from the approval of others." (Wilding, 2020)

Your personal mission statement should be positive with a focus on what you want and not on what you don't want.

To be truly effective, it should be no longer than three sentences using simple and straightforward language.

It's worthwhile to take the time to think about why you want to stop gambling and how you want to feel moving forward.

Here is mine:

> "To live each day with purpose, honesty, and clear intent so that I can experience inner peace, financial stability, and self-respect. I will do this by setting goals and taking action with a specific focus on my mind, body, and spirit."

Block Online Gambling Sites

Because of their instant availability, online gambling sites are the most dangerous. Thankfully there is gambling-specific software available that will block access to all gambling sites. The list below is worth exploring to find the best option for you. Some are available for free whilst others only have a paid option.

GamBan (UK residents can get free license)
https://www.gamban.com

Gamblock (Windows computers and Android phones)
https://gamblock.com

BetBlocker (Windows, Linux and Mac)
https://www.betblocker.org

Netnanny - Netnanny is a general blocking software and has capability on Windows computers, ioS, and Android phones.
https://www.netnanny.com

Block Gambling Transactions in Your Banking App

Many banks have the facility to block deposits to gambling sites within their app. This adds another layer of protection for you, and most cannot be reversed without first having a discussion with Customer Support.

Join a Self-Exclusion Program

A self-exclusion program allows you to exclude yourself from gambling facilities in your country. Depending upon your location these programs will work differently, however, most give you the choice of the duration of your self-exclusion. This means that during that time you will not be able to access your casino accounts. When checking the details, ensure that the casino where your account is located is on the list of excluded casinos. If not, then contact that casino directly and opt-in to their own self-exclusion program.

Connect with Your Spiritual Side

As mentioned previously, this was a key component in my own recovery. This is not about religion, per se, but rather being in touch with the spirit within you and practicing self-love.

A good start to this is forgiveness. It's important to move forward with positive energy and guilt and recrimination are not helpful. Be compassionate and kind to yourself because you are worth it.

There are billions of people on our planet and yet still there was the need to create you. You are a unique individual with qualities, talents, and dreams like no other. You are here for a reason even if you don't know what that is.

Don't let your past define who you are or who you can be. By connecting with your inner being you will find the strength you need to succeed in overcoming your addiction as well as a deep love for yourself that you have never experienced before.

When you feel this love, your actions towards yourself will be made with love, and when you act with love you will have no regrets.

Write Letters from Your Future Self

I know this may sound like you will be doing something the wrong way around. After all, today you are still you, a gambling addict, so how can you write to your current self from your gambling-free future self?

This is far easier than it sounds. First, you need to create your future self in your mind. Think about the qualities she has. How does she act? What does she believe in? How does she spend her days? What are her strengths and weaknesses? How does she see herself?

This is a powerful exercise as it allows you to focus on the positive you *you* want to be, rather than the you who you are now, with all your negative baggage.

Give her the best parts of yourself because even with all the negativity you have experienced, there are wonderful parts of you that you can use as a foundation for creating your future self.

Of course, she is not a compulsive gambler and when you write to yourself from her point of view those words will encourage and motivate you. Then begin to make decisions from her perspective as your future self has clarity of thought and peace of mind.

She can trust herself and her judgment and her decisions will be in her best interests and consequently, that means they will be in your best interests too.

You know what you need to hear today. Only you know deep down what words will resonate with you and make the difference. This is your opportunity to hear the words you've been longing to hear and believe me because they are actually from you, they will be more impactful than anything another could say to you.

She is on your side.

Now it's time for you to be on hers.

Take a Holistic Approach

Your gambling addiction is the symptom of a bigger problem. This is the symptom of an underlying issue. As your gambling issue has had a negative impact on many aspects of your life, so should your recovery focus on different areas of your life.

"The holistic approach to addiction recovery is based on the idea that this type of problem occurs because you are out of balance. In other words, there is at least one area of your life that is preventing you from experiencing the happiness you deserve and is, instead, driving you into addictive behaviors. The goal then is to restore you to balance, not only so you can break free of alcohol or drug abuse, but more importantly, so you can live a wonderful life." (6 Benefits of Choosing a Holistic Approach to Addiction Recovery, 2014)

By taking a holistic approach to your recovery, you will be ensuring that all aspects of yourself are treated by focusing on your mind, your body, and your soul for optimum wellness and balance.

In simplistic terms, this means improving your diet, exercise, sleep, and water intake to improve your overall health and vitality in general. Approach the way you usually do things differently. Adopt a new attitude, learn new things and stop repeating patterns from the past and be grateful for what you have today. Get to know your inner being and learn to listen to that voice that has your best interests at heart.

Work on Your Finances

For a long time, your finances have been neglected. As hard as it may be, if you haven't already done so, you need to figure out your starting point today. This doesn't mean you necessarily need to go back and figure out how much you've spent on gambling as this can be counter-productive.

What you need to do is get your bank balance today and the balances of your credit cards. Work out exactly what you need to live on and what your expected income should be. Then start working on a plan to get yourself financially stable.

It's a good idea to start by reducing any credit card debts you have as the higher the amounts you owe are, the more you will be paying in interest each month.

You may need to look for an additional source of income and something that I used which would pay approximately 10 USD per test is a site called User Testing. This can bring you an approximate extra 300 USD per month depending on how many tests you complete, all from the comfort of your own home.

Don't let the word test put you off. This is actually fun and is a legitimate way of making money online where you get to give your opinion on websites that are in development. You get to help brands create better products and experiences for their customers around the world.

These tests vary in length. Some take less than five minutes, others about twenty and there are also interviews that pay between 30 - 60 USD. All you have to do is open a free account, download the software, complete a practice test and then browse the available tests each day. You will not be suitable for all tests, and you will find days where there is nothing, but this balances with other days where you can complete loads.

After each test, you can see the amount that is due to you and exactly seven days to the hour after the test upload, you will receive payment via PayPal.

If you think this is something that may help you earn extra money, go to https://www.usertesting.com/get-paid-to-test

As long as you have a plan and stick to it, financial stability can be achieved with the money you will save from gambling. It may take time but as each month passes, this will get better and better, and you will feel better and better too.

"The best time to start was yesterday. The next best time is now." - Anonymous

Chapter 9

Your Future is Now

"The only person you are destined to become is the person you decide to be." - Ralph Waldo Emerson

THERE WAS YOU.

Then there was you and your GAM.

You can continue like this, or you can bring in another force to help you overcome the thoughts your GAM puts in your head. You need help to argue with your GAM, as you have not been able to do this successfully yourself, hence you have become a compulsive gambler, completely at the mercy of your GAM.

Bring in your future self.

Future Self

Your future self is not a compulsive gambler. Your future self has the qualities you want in life. Your future self is strong, determined, and has her own real interests at heart. Your future self is not easily persuaded or fooled and doesn't fall for the mind games your GAM plays on you. Your future self wants you to succeed because her very existence in the future is dependent upon your actions today. She is your ally. This is who you can count on. This is who you can trust.

Your future self is not weighed down by feelings of guilt or shame. She feels free to explore her potential fully and embrace who she is without recrimination. Her vibe is good. Her attitude is positive.

A compulsive gambler is an exact opposite. They can pretend to be these things, but deep down they know they are not. They will never reach their potential or get to know who or what they could really be.

A successful person will make the tough choices with the most positive and beneficial end result in mind. They will trust their own judgment and trust themselves to do the right thing.

A compulsive gambler makes choices that are harmful whilst looking for that quick fix. Not only do they lie to others about how much time they gamble, how much they spend etc., but they also lie to themselves.

Not being able to trust yourself is one of the biggest obstacles you will have to achieve real things in life.

Your future self will plan and think about the future and what the actions of today mean. A compulsive gambler dares not think about this. They are even too scared to look at their bank account, except for the balance to see how much they have to spend. They won't add up the money they've lost.

Just as you allowed your GAM to take over your life, you now need to replace your GAM with your future self. Your future self is not a parasite, and you are not simply the host. Your future self is you, but the very best version of you and will make the very best decisions on your behalf so that you can finally enjoy your best life.

Why You'll Never Be Happy with a Gambling Addiction

I know you've heard the expressions before that happiness comes from within. Happiness is an inside job, and believe me, I have found this to be true.

But what exactly does this mean and how does it relate to your gambling addiction?

I am talking about deep happiness where you experience that joy for life. This is different from feeling temporary happiness from being involved in an activity or affected by someone else.

These are all from the external world. And as much as we need our external world to be good, this does not guarantee happiness. We've all heard of the stories of the wealthy being desperately unhappy with some well-known personalities even taking their own lives.

We often wonder about this because to the outside world they seemed to have it all, yet still, they weren't happy. External happiness is not real. It's not sustainable. Being outwardly comfortable does not translate to inner comfort and often serves only to mask the underlying problem.

As mentioned previously, my own path to recovery was successful once I connected with my inner being. Another way to describe this feeling is worthiness. I went from self-loathing to feeling worthy and relevant.

And when you feel worthy, your behavior changes in ways you could never imagine.

From Mindless to Mindful

For far too long you have been automated and acting irresponsibly without any thought to the harm you were causing yourself or others. There are times when you tried to do the right thing because you knew your addiction was wrong but were still helpless to act differently.

You are no longer going to be mindless. In other words, you are no longer going to act without thought. Also, you are going to start working on the way you think in all areas of your life.

You may be surprised to learn that you are not your thoughts. Just because you think a thought, doesn't mean you have to go with it. Random thoughts can come into our heads all the time and we don't have to own them. They are just thoughts.

However, you need to focus on deliberate thought. This is being mindful of what you think. Think thoughts that make you feel good to rewire your brain into shaping your belief system to impact you and your actions in a positive manner.

Here are some examples of what I mean:

Random Thought: *I am not good enough.*

Deliberate Thought: *Even though my actions up till now have not been good for me, I am good enough.*

Learn how to dismiss negative thoughts and replace them with thoughts that will make you feel better. This is not about lying to yourself, as there's been enough deceit already, but rather rephrasing a thought, so it is both honest and helpful.

What we think impacts how we feel. When we think negatively, we feel miserable, but when we think positively, our emotions become positive and when we feel positive in general are actions are positive too.

You Deserve More

It's important to understand that you are not what's happened to you in your past. Nor are you your actions and you should not define yourself by either of these. You are so much more.

You are a special soul who has simply lost touch with the essence of who you really are. However, somewhere deep within yourself, you know this to be true.

You deserve so much more than what you've been experiencing. For this to happen, you first need to rid yourself of the unnecessary and heavy baggage that you're carrying.

It's time to live light.

Find Your Worth

When you feel worthless you will not feel the need to make the change. I mean, what difference will it make? You won't believe that anything you do will be effective. You won't believe that the required effort will be worthwhile because you don't feel worthwhile.

But you are worthwhile, and your effort will be too.

When you finally accept that you are worth the effort and that you have what you need within you, your recovery will be closer and much easier than you currently believe.

Your beliefs are built on your thoughts. What you keep telling yourself is what you come to believe.

So, start thinking that you are worthy because you most definitely are. Your future self letters will help you see this.

Your recovery journey will be unique and special to you. It might begin today, tomorrow or next month, but whenever it starts, you may initially still feel the urge to gamble so it's important to have practical steps to action to calm your gambling urges should they arise.

Chapter 10

Calm Your Urges

"Start by doing what's necessary, then what's possible; and suddenly you are doing the impossible."
- Saint Francis of Assisi

RECOVERY IS A JOURNEY, and during that journey, you will experience highs and lows. Although it's not an easy journey, it is probably the most worthwhile and rewarding one you will ever take.

Depending upon how you decide to stop, you will experience varying degrees of temptation resulting in that internal battle with your GAM or feelings of negativity.

It's important to think about this possibility so you can expect it, to plan and prepare for it.

If you choose to stop suddenly and quickly, and implement the steps laid out in the chapter Time for Action, Tomorrow, you most likely won't experience the internal battle with your GAM because there is nothing to be conflicted about as you will have been cut off from all casinos.

However, you may experience "buyer's remorse" and regret the drastic and irreversible steps you took. You may also feel lost or anxious about this decision, but this is more about what you think you will feel than what you will actually feel.

Don't be disheartened. Remember, you are focusing on healing in full and not just recovering from the symptom of your dis-ease.

If you do experience these feelings, they will pass faster than you expect, and you will begin to notice how calm you feel because you are not conflicted.

This is similar to those moments of clarity you've experienced before in those in-between gambling sessions, but this time, the GAM isn't coming back, and you can breathe again and take comfort that you took that brave step and did the right thing.

If you decide you are not yet ready to implement the Tomorrow steps and want to first complete Today and work on the steps outlined in the Ongoing section, that is fine too.

However, this means that you are still extremely vulnerable to your GAM, because there is still something to be conflicted about.

Even if your mission is to stop gambling, if there is even the slightest chance that you could give in to your GAM, your GAM will be there pulling out all the tricks.

This is where the Pre Gambling questions can be effective. If you can't commit to stopping gambling today, at least commit to completing those questions before any and every gambling session and also complete the part that provides reflection after gambling.

But even before doing that, as hard as it is with your GAM in your head, look at your Mission Statement and follow the plan you have prepared for that moment.

Ideas to Calm Your Urges

If you've made the conscious decision to stop gambling and are determined to make the effort, then the practical steps listed below will be helpful.

It is important that these are implemented in the moments of clarity that occur between the gambling sessions where you are in control and your GAM is dormant.

These ideas and practical tips will help you recover over time if you are not able to quit immediately. However, none of the tips below will make any difference in your recovery if you don't really want to quit, and your GAM will come up with many reasons and excuses to avoid you taking the necessary steps.

Some of the ideas are designed to help you rewire your brain by giving you something else to think about. Some are to help you face the reality of the situation to effect immediate change and some are to help you occupy yourself in a different way.

I suggest you select a few ideas from the list below and get started with them right away.

Change Your Routine

Make changes to your daily routine, especially for the times you are most vulnerable. We have discussed replacing your GAM with your future self. Gradually, your future self will take back control. So, what did your future self do today to become who she will be?

- Did she do a course to expand her knowledge and potential income?

- Did she start going to the gym?

- Did she give up other bad habits?

- Did she join a club or take up a new hobby?

- Did she work on mending her relationships?

Instead of spending money and time on gambling, does she get pleasure from shopping and buying new clothes, makeup, and jewelry? (This is not to substitute one problem for another.) Often compulsive gamblers don't spend money on these things because it is all going to gambling - here you can make a conscious choice to rather spend the money on something else and feel the benefit of it.

Pay Bills Immediately

Pay all your bills on the day you get paid. If you have direct debits set up, change the dates of these to the day after you get paid. Once this is done, go to the store and buy all the non-perishable items you will need until your next paycheck comes in.

By doing this you are taking care of two things. Firstly, you will reduce the stress of not having money for bills because you spent it on gambling. You will have what you need at home to survive with cleaning, personal hygiene and non-perishable food essentials. Your monthly commitments will be paid and you are reducing the money you have for gambling.

This becomes another barrier.

Secondly, you will begin to feel in control and experience positive feelings from doing the right thing.

Tell Somebody

If you've been a secretive gambler, this can be a terrifying thought but if you choose the right person (friend, family member, or even a Gambling group), this will bring your dark secret into the light. This way you will be held accountable in the future and also have support when you need it most. It is important that you choose who to tell wisely. You don't want to make a bad situation worse by feeling judged or to have this thrown in your face which would have the potential to derail your recovery.

Keep Your Hands Busy

If you are an online gambler who usually uses your phone to gamble in online casinos, you get used to having something in your hands to play. Find a game, something like Candy Crush, and satisfy your need to do something with your hands.

Better still, learn to knit or crochet. I found crocheting calming and the advantage of this is that you have something to show for it. I knew nothing about crocheting so I watched a few YouTube videos and picked something simple like a blanket to try. As your blanket gets bigger and bigger this is a visual representation of your success in not gambling.

Another idea is to purchase some adult coloring books, pens and pencils and occupy your hands by creating beautiful images. You will find a large variety to choose from with all sorts of themes and detail, so even if you thought coloring books were only for children, you will be surprised at what is available for you.

Make Extra Money Instead

Use your gambling time to rather make extra money instead. Over time this will build up. You will have gone from depleting your bank account to increasing your bank balance. You can get a part-time job that will fill up those gambling hours, break your routine and improve your finances.

I've already mentioned a site I used to make some extra money, but you can even take this a step further. Could it be time to start a side hustle? Maybe you already have a talent that if focused on, you could make money from.

Stop Being Mocked

Earlier on in the book, you discovered how you have been manipulated by the casinos to keep depositing money. Now let's take that one step further. Visualize a person in the casino laughing at you every time you make a deposit. They laugh at you and behind the scenes and call you a sucker, but to your face, they smile, and make you feel welcome and special.

You are not a sucker and it's time to stop allowing yourself to be treated like one.

Reconcile Your Bank Account

You may find this one difficult. It's extremely hard to look at the cost of your actions in black and white. Although it's a good idea to understand exactly what you've spent, this can be extremely shocking because there will be no denying the hard truth.

You will discover that your estimate is probably far less, and this is because you've been in denial and if you'd faced the truth before, you might have stopped.

It's important you do this when you have worked on your mindset first. The last thing I want is for you to see the shocking truth and be overcome with guilt and shame. That will be counter-productive and could set off another downhill spiral.

Develop an Attitude of Gratitude

When we are grateful for everything we have, no matter what it is, we are leaving no room for emptiness.

When we develop an attitude of gratitude, we become accustomed to being thankful for everything, including things we usually take for granted.

Be grateful for the hot water in your shower, the roof over your head, and the food on your plate. Notice the sound of the rain and the beauty of nature. Pay attention to the people who love you and give that love back. Be grateful to have these people in your life, even if there are issues with them that need working out.

Be thankful for your inner strength and the abilities you have, even if you've misused them before. Be thankful you have today and a future worth striving for.

Be grateful for being you.

The more grateful you are, the more you will have to be grateful for.

By consciously having a spirit of thanks you will feel different inside and when you feel different inside, you will act differently.

Affirmations and Prayer

Affirmations and prayer are highly effective and serve different purposes. Affirmations can be used as a method to reinforce your commitment and motivation. They can be inspiring and helpful.

One of my favorite affirmations is from Robin Banks:

> *"I am Brilliant I am Bright*
> *I am a Radiant Being of Light*
> *I am an Outstanding Peak Performer*
> *I am a Dynamic Life Transformer"*
> (Banks, 2016)

This affirmation connected with me on a deep level and encapsulated everything I needed and was going through. Not only did this include my connection with my spiritual being, but the determination and conviction that I felt within to turn my life around.

It rolls off the tongue beautifully and is so easy to remember. I would walk around the house repeating this over and over.

We all know the power of prayer.

When you connect with your higher power it is truly a humbling and uplifting experience. Use this time to express your gratitude, ask for guidance and strength and honestly express yourself.

Prayer has a calming effect that can influence our thoughts and the way we feel. As you go through your recovery journey, it is important to feel grounded and connected, to have that inner strength and wisdom for making tough decisions to implement the required changes.

Start a Journal

Journaling is not only therapeutic but also provides an opportunity for you to keep track of your feelings and thoughts. Entries can be as frequent as you want them to be with no rules or quotas to fill. Simply write down what's going on in your life and how you're coping.

Be honest with your words as they should be for your eyes only.

When you express yourself on paper, you're able to make more sense of what's going on. This allows you to focus on what's important, find solutions to challenges and reflect on your progress.

If you've never kept a journal before, then introducing this new activity into your life will take up some of your time and become part of a new routine you can enjoy.

Keep a Gambling Logbook

I know you have a lot to work through and might not be quite ready to quit today. However, if you are going to gamble, then do your utmost to change the way you do it. I've already asked you to commit to completing the Pre Gambling Questions, but additionally, it is important that you face up to the reality of what you're doing and a good way to do this is to keep a Gambling Logbook.

This way you can record when and where you gamble and the amount you spend. It doesn't have to be complicated. You just need to keep track, so you are precisely aware of what this is costing you. Being in black and white, although perhaps difficult to face, you will not be in denial and the hard truth may be the final convincer that you need to take action.

Count the Days

Make yourself a dated wall chart and cross off each day that is gambling-free. I suggest using three colors, green, red and black. For days that were easy to handle, draw a green cross, and for those days in which you struggle but still coped, draw a red cross. On the days your GAM got the better of you, draw a black cross.

The idea here is to have a visual representation of your gambling-free days with the goal of extending that duration each time.

You can extend it by a day or double it. This gives you an actual goal to focus on and a sense of accomplishment when you meet the objective.

Of course, if you've already implemented the steps not to gamble, you can do this slightly differently. Instead of drawing a cross, write down the money you saved by not gambling.

In a short time, you will see the impact your choice has made. Then at the end of the month transfer that money into a savings account or pay it into your credit card accounts to reduce any debt your gambling incurred.

Enjoy the Simple Things in Life

This is the perfect time to start enjoying the simple things in life that you probably have ignored for a long time. Get close to nature. Take a walk on the beach if you live on the coast. Enjoy the sounds of the water and smell of the sea. Go camping. Go swimming. Ride a bike. Get a pet. Sit in the sun.

Buy some flowers and take pleasure in arranging them. Change your hairstyle. Buy yourself a new pocketbook or wallet to signify your new commitment to your financial responsibility.

Learn to make ice cream and enjoy eating it. Grow some vegetables. Write poetry. Explore your neighborhood.

Smile more.

Spend time doing things that you haven't done in a while, if ever.

Start to take pleasure in simple activities.

It's time to stop and smell the roses.

Chapter 11

Feel Like a True Winner

"All the suffering, stress and addiction comes from not realizing you already are what you are looking for."
- Jon Kabat-Zin

IF YOU CAN'T TRUST yourself, who can you trust?

What I hated the most about being a compulsive gambler was the inability to trust myself. As we all know, trust is fundamental to any successful and happy relationship and that includes the relationship you have with yourself.

It's difficult to live life when you can't trust your own judgment or believe in yourself. In life we are encouraged to be positive, to see the glass half full as opposed to half-empty, and this is another thing your GAM feeds on.

You want to be a winner in life, not just at the casino where you are never the winner. Even when you win at the casino it is just a fleeting moment and probably will never be an amount that exceeds the money you have deposited and lost over time.

There are exceptions to this. Some people have won mega jackpots with life-changing consequences, but these are the *exceptions*. This is a concept your GAM will use against you, after all, it could be you too. Why not you? That person is no more special, no more deserving than you are, and it happened to them.

We all want to feel special and worthy. We see a casino win as a blessing, a sign from up above that we are not just another loser or statistic. We are different. We are special. We are winners.

This is like dog racing, also known as greyhound racing, which is the racing of greyhounds on an enclosed track while they pursue an electrically controlled and propelled mechanical hare - always in front of you, being chased but never being reached.

This is all part of the illusion.

You need to have the wins that are real for you. You need to believe in yourself and your abilities. You are good enough. You can tap into the magic that is within you, that you were born with, to create a life you are proud of so that you can live in peace and in harmony with who you are.

In an earlier chapter, I discussed the importance of self-image, self-esteem, and self-confidence in living a happy and harmonious life.

By separating yourself from your GAM, I explained how you would get temporary relief. You need to put the work in so that you can benefit from a positive and healthy self-image so that your self-esteem and self-confidence are aligned with your vision of yourself in the long run.

Redefining Your Life on Your Terms

It's time to redefine yourself so that you no longer see yourself as a gambler. When you see yourself differently, so will others.

You need to find what I call your "soul purpose".

By this I mean discovering what it is that brings you inner joy. Inner joy is the key to real happiness. Once you find that key and begin to use it, you will become your future self.

Your future self will no longer be an idea or a concept to strive for. You will become the best version of yourself.

This is not supposed to be overwhelming and remember, as you read this today, you are reading it from the perspective of where you are now and not from the perspective of where you want to be. But when you begin implementing everything you've learned, you will feel inspired to find your "soul purpose", and when you reconnect with your inner being, you will be shown the way.

Able to Heal Emotionally

Let go of your self-loathing, self-judgment, and emotional numbness and replace those negative and harmful attributes with empathy, self-compassion, and kindness for yourself.

This you do by getting to the root cause of your dis-ease once and for all. Go to therapy, talk about it, explore your feelings, and learn to accept your past so that you no longer have to suffer those consequences in the present or future.

You don't need to suffer anymore. It's impossible to change the past but you have the capability to change how you deal with it. Although we may not be able to control everything that happens to us in our lives, we can control how we react. We can learn how to react in ways that are not harmful to us.

Self-forgiveness is paramount. The pain you've been feeling and the actions you took to escape only compounded your pain. Your actions were not out of malice. You did not set out to cause turmoil in your life and it's time to accept this and treat yourself with the empathy you deserve.

It's time to forgive yourself.

Higher Self-Confidence

As you progress in your recovery journey, you will become more self-confident. Knowing you have been through something as difficult as gambling addiction and made it through will remind you that you can get through other tough times too.

And there will be tough times because that is the nature of life. But a tough time can just be a tough time. It doesn't have to evolve into a tough life.

With hindsight, you will begin to see this more clearly. You will have confidence in your ability to make difficult decisions and you will begin to trust your own judgment once again.

And as life presents you with more opportunities to demonstrate this, the higher your self-confidence will become, and with higher self-confidence comes the ability to go beyond your comfort zone and reach your full potential.

Working Toward a Better You

If you want to become the very best version of yourself, you need to explore what this could possibly be. Redirecting your time and money into developing new skills that you can use to shape your future and create real success is something you have to do.

You want to be able to say "I did that" with pride. This doesn't have to be a daunting experience and can be more than one thing.

It doesn't need to be something huge, only something that pushes you out of your comfort zone and challenges the beliefs you hold about yourself to bring you personal satisfaction.

You can start off with something small and progress over time. Or you can jump straight in and go for it right away.

I know there is something within you just like I finally found something within me. That something was always within me, but I didn't know it. I didn't feel it. I didn't even consider it.

And how could I when my sole focus was on my gambling addiction? Being all consumed with gambling boxes you into a reality that isn't real. Your real reality is what's always been buried deep inside you, under your dis-ease.

You have always carried that seed but without nurturing it, it has never had the opportunity to blossom.

Let your inner light shine on that seed even if you have difficulty believing that it's there. Every step you take to distance yourself from your gambling addiction and resolve your dis-ease, will be like watering and providing nutrients to that beautiful seed.

As time moves forward that seed will begin to sprout and when it does you will be able to feel it more easily and begin to blossom.

And when you feel it, you will become more excited and optimistic about your life than any casino win was ever able to give you.

You will finally feel like a true winner.

Chapter 12

Help and Support

"You are the only one who can make it happen for you. Others can support and encourage you, but you have to find the energy within in order to step into the center of your own life and take charge." - Lynda Field

YOUR RECOVERY IS DOWN to you.

Recovery isn't going to happen without you making the conscious decision to stop gambling and get your life back on track.

Even though you will be doing this for yourself, and the decision will be yours alone to make, that doesn't mean you have to go through the recovery process alone.

If you need support and encouragement, there are plenty of resources that you can benefit from depending on your location and needs.

Here you will find resources listed by location. If your location is not listed, then visit the Gamblers Anonymous link below, under the International section, to find the resource in your country.

International

RecoverMe App
RecoverMe is a mobile application designed to help addicted gamblers. This app was specifically designed with the help of psychologists, psychiatrists and also those suffering from gambling addiction.

Download from the Apple App store https://apple.co/3wgSaYL

Download from the Google Play store https://bit.ly/3PxkcGi

Gamblers Anonymous
Gamblers Anonymous is a fellowship of people who share their experiences, strengths, and hopes to solve their common problems to help each other recover from gambling addiction

https://gamblersanonymous.org

To find help for the country you're in go to: https://gamblersanonymous.org/ga/addresses

United States of America

Algamus Gambling Treatment
Algamus provides the only JCAHO-accredited gambling specific residential treatment program in the USA.
https://www.algamus.org
637 W. Hillside Avenue, Prescott AZ 86301
algamus@aol.com
888-527-3098

GamTalk
Online support for gambling issues.
https://www.gamtalk.org

NCPG - National Council on Problem Gambling
Operator of the National Problem Gambling Helpline Network.
https://www.ncpgambling.org/
https://www.ncpgambling.org/chat
1-800-522-4700

Promises Behavioral Health Addiction Treatment Centers
Comprehensive, evidence-based addiction treatment centers with locations nationwide offering both residential and outpatient programs.
https://www.promises.com
103 Powell Court, Suite 100, Brentwood, TN 37027
1-888 967-9140

United Kingdom

GamCare
Treatment and support for problem gamblers.
https://www.gamcare.org.uk
info@gamcare.org.uk
0808 8020 133

NHS National Problem Gambling Clinic
Help and support for gambling addiction.
https://bit.ly/3AURAmn
ncba.cnwl@nhs.net
020 7381 7722

Gordon Moody

A leading UK charity dedicated to providing support and treatment for addicted gamblers.

https://gordonmoody.org.uk

help@gordonmoody.org.uk

01384 241292

Other Regions

Australia

Gambling Help Online
https://www.gamblinghelponline.org.au

Canada

Responsible Gambling Council
https://www.responsiblegambling.org

Finland

Peluuri
https://www.peluuri.fi

Ireland

Extern Problem Gambling
https://www.problemgambling.ie

Singapore

Singapore Counselling Centre
https://scc.sg/e/gambling-addiction

South Africa

South African Responsible Gambling Foundation
https://responsiblegambling.org.za

Conclusion

"If you chased your recovery like you chased your high, you would never relapse again." - Unknown

I DO BUY AN occasional lottery ticket when the amount is exceptionally high, but only one and only occasionally, which is what I think most people do. This is good for me because I feel normal when doing this and this has nothing to do with compulsive behavior.

Casinos can only take from you what you give them. When you stop giving them, they will stop taking from you. And when they stop taking from you, you will no longer be stressed and feel that awful guilt from losing.

The example below is very obvious and basic, but please look at it. When you read it in this moment of clarity, it will feel different from when you are actually in the casino, with your GAM whispering in your ear.

You go to the casino with $100 and you load it into a slot machine. You start playing. Before you know it, half of it has gone. You start feeling a little anxious because you really can't afford to lose that money and you haven't been there very long.

Then three scatter symbols appear, and you've got that elusive free spin. This turns out to be really good because you get a spin in a spin. As you watch the tally of the winnings rise, you are pleased because you now have more than what you started with.

So far so good.

As you feel lady luck is on your side, you increase your bet. Your machine is hot. Then the usual happens. The slot machine takes back everything you won in your free spin. You believe it's got to turn around, so you continue.

But that was it. There are no more spins, no beautiful lines. Nothing. You've lost your $100 and have to do battle as to whether you should withdraw more money and try your luck again.

You do this. Now you have withdrawn $200 and have already lost half of that. I don't need to tell you what happens next because it's all too familiar to you.

Don't start thinking about the exceptions when you did win. Yes, I know it can happen and it happened to me too, but those are the exceptions and even when you have a reasonably good win, that win does not exceed all the money you've spent over time.

And when you get that big win, what do you do? Do you cash out and go home happy with your money or do you push your luck even further?

I know what you do.

You see, it's not about the money. If that was your goal, in that session when you won and were ahead, you would walk away. But what you - or rather, your GAM is after, is to repeat that feeling.

Aren't you just tired of this? I know I was. So, when did I realize it was finally over?

My last gambling session was online and that time it felt different. I felt different. Even though I was playing my favorite game, I was not fully engaged, and nor did I feel that usual rush. My mind kept wondering with thoughts on other things I could rather be doing. This had a positive effect on me and for the first time ever, I actually logged out with a little money left in my account.

This was different from logging out with the intention of coming back later to play out the money that would still be available. This was not a lot of money, so nothing really to come back for, but more importantly I did not feel compelled to carry on till my funds were completely depleted even though I could have continued to play for a short while more.

This was an active decision. I had had enough. I was bored. The thrill was gone. I was finding more and more satisfaction in other areas of my life since I had made the decision to start my recovery journey and had implemented the necessary steps to ensure success.

But how did I know for sure? How did I know that wasn't a once-off experience and that my GAM would be back with its usual bag of tricks?

Although I felt it was all over, it was only when I had the opportunity to prove it to myself by making a decision I had never made before.

About a week after my last gambling session, I received a notification from a casino offering me free gaming credits. Prior to this, I was always over the moon to receive free gaming credits as it gave me the opportunity to gamble without initially risking my own money. I say initially because I would always start with the casino credits and inevitably, when they were gone, being in that zone, I would deposit my own money. And of course, this is what the casinos want you to do!

However, on this occasion, I ignored the offer. My GAM no longer had control over me, and the casino was not able to manipulate me into making decisions that I would regret.

I had slayed my GAM!

By finally dealing with my root problem, there was nothing there for my GAM to hold onto. This, together with the practical steps I implemented, my spiritual connection and my increased self-confidence and determination to live a different life, is what finally set me free.

Isn't it worth believing that perhaps there is something else you can do that will give you a really good feeling? But how will you ever know, if you have a one-track mind with no room for anything else?

The goal of your recovery is to slay your GAM and remove yourself from the havoc it creates in your life.

Remember, your GAM is only effective when you have the ability to gamble. Once you remove this ability, your GAM will no longer be able to feed off you. It will no longer have any control over you and won't be able to feed your brain with thoughts that are not based on logic.

You will permanently be free of the roller-coaster ride.

And even if it takes you a while to find it, the bonus is that you will have peace of mind and not carry that terrible burden that stems from gambling anymore. Of course, you may still have to deal with your dis-ease, but at least your thinking will no longer be clouded and you will be able to move forward.

Believe me, you've got this. With the power of your inner being and the perspective and attitude of your future self together with your own determination to change your life, you will have all the tools and resources you need to create the life you deserve.

Please understand that your gambling addiction is only a chapter of your life. It's not your whole story. It's not the complete book. You get to still write your ending and only you can decide what words your final chapter will include.

The day will come soon when you promise yourself enough is enough. No more.

And you will mean it. You will be able to trust it, and trust yourself, because you'll never have to make that promise again.

After all this time and everything you've been through, you get to have the last word and in doing so, finally keep your word to yourself and fulfill your desire to win.

References

6 Benefits of choosing a holistic approach to addiction recovery. (2014, April 17). UK Rehab. https://bit.ly/3AmpsXV

Banks, R. (2016, November 22). *Robin Banks - I am brilliant I am bright.* Facebook. https://bit.ly/3QLWpU7

Cherry, K. (2022, July 29). *What Is cognitive dissonance?* Very Well Mind. https://bit.ly/3zYQGUd

Collier, R. (2008, July 15). *Gambling treatment options: A roll of the dice.* National Library of Medicine. https://bit.ly/3SnS1b1

Definition of parasite. (2022, August 6). Merriam-Webster. https://bit.ly/3dDoOgD

Eisen, S. A., Lin, N., Lyons M J, & Scherrer, J. F. (1998, September). *Familial influences on gambling behavior: An analysis of 3359 twin pairs.* National Library of Medicine. https://bit.ly/3PJssmR

Faillace, L. A. (2021, June 25). *How we see ourselves.* UTHealth Houston.
https://bit.ly/3Qvltz3

Hollingshead, S. J., Wohl, M. J., & Davis, C. G. (2021, July 21). *On being loyal to a casino: The interactive influence of tier status and disordered gambling symptomatology on attitudinal and behavioral loyalty.*
National Library of Medicine.
https://bit.ly/3prFVok

Host (biology). (2022, May 20).
Wikipedia.
https://bit.ly/3zYRmsJ

Is gambling hereditary? (n.d.).
Gateway Foundation.
https://bit.ly/3c1fEu4

Kumar, B. (n.d.). *The outer world is nothing but a true reflection of our inner world.*
The Spiritual Journey.
https://bit.ly/3KhJzLr

Michels, B., & Stutz, P. (2017). *Five steps for overcoming fear.*
Goop.
https://bit.ly/3C7VI3n

Salters-Pedneault, PhD, K. (2021, April 6). *Types and symptoms of common psychiatric disorders.*
Verywell Mind.
https://bit.ly/3duC6Mp

Samaritans new guidelines equip gambling businesses to do more to prevent suicide. (2021, April 27).
Samaritans.
https://bit.ly/3JYcaVQ

The science behind gambling. (n.d.).
Responsible Gambling Council.
https://bit.ly/3CbBndr

Statistics of gambling addiction 2016. (n.d.).
North American Foundation for Gambling Addiction Help.
https://bit.ly/3SRj1Vb

Slutske, W. S. (2006, February 1). *Natural Recovery and Treatment-Seeking in Pathological Gambling: Results of Two U.S. National Surveys.*
The American Journal of Psychiatry.
https://bit.ly/3OWcuVl

Wilding, M. (2020, November 9). *Why you need a personal mission statement.*
Forbes.
https://bit.ly/3w9Dv1C

Wiley, C. (2020, September 24). *Is there such a thing as healthy anger?*
Talk Space.
https://bit.ly/3bYk5Wr

Lightning Source UK Ltd.
Milton Keynes UK
UKHW010804211222
414213UK00001B/101